Activating Your
TRUE IDENTITY

Activating Your

TRUE IDENTITY

LEARNING THE UPGRADE PRINCIPLE

Written by:

DR. LON AND LAURIE STETTLER

FORWARD BY LARRY BURGBACHER

XULON PRESS

Xulon Press
2301 Lucien Way #415
Maitland, FL 32751
407.339.4217
www.xulonpress.com

© 2023 by Dr. Lon and Laurie Stettler

All rights reserved solely by the author. The author guarantees all contents are original and do not infringe upon the legal rights of any other person or work. No part of this book may be reproduced in any form without the permission of the author.

Due to the changing nature of the Internet, if there are any web addresses, links, or URLs included in this manuscript, these may have been altered and may no longer be accessible. The views and opinions shared in this book belong solely to the author and do not necessarily reflect those of the publisher. The publisher therefore disclaims responsibility for the views or opinions expressed within the work.

Unless otherwise indicated, Scripture quotations taken from the New American Standard Bible (NASB). Copyright © 1995 by The Lockman Foundation. Used by permission. All rights reserved.

Unless otherwise indicated, Scripture quotations taken from the New King James Version (NKJV). Copyright © 1982 by Thomas Nelson, Inc. Used by permission. All rights reserved.

Unless otherwise indicated, Scripture quotations taken from The Message (MSG). Copyright © 1993, 1994, 1995, 1996, 2000, 2001, 2002. Used by permission of NavPress Publishing Group. Used by permission. All rights reserved.

Paperback ISBN-13: 978-1-6628-7047-7
Ebook ISBN-13: 978-1-6628-7048-4

Endorsements

I have known Dr. Lon Stettler for over thirty-five years. When I tell you that he is a student of the Word, that is a gross understatement. His insight in helping the reader discover who they are in Christ is refreshing and invigorating. The most foundational principles in following Christ include the discoveries that we are loved, chosen, accepted, adopted, secure, and significant. Do yourself a favor and dive into this book with an open heart and mind. You won't regret it.

Brad Rosenberg, Chief Partnership Office, Convoy of Hope, Springfield, MO

I have enjoyed getting to know Lon Stettler and hearing his heart and teaching over the past couple of years here at Faith Church. There are so many road blocks in discovering your true identity in Christ. *Activating Your True Identity* shows us the perspective shift that every believer needs to experience on what it truly means to be loved by your Creator. I love the practical 33 activating points and prayers that literally lift and rid the spirit of condemnation and awaken our born-again spirit! As you read this book you will discover what the Bible really says about who you are in Christ, and the practical ways to live and initiate a life of faith!

Jason Burgbacher, Executive Pastor, Faith Church, Summerville SC

I highly recommend Dr. Lon Stettler's book as a roadmap to a deeper spiritual life. This book gave me a deeper realization of who I am in Christ. I was challenged by "responding with faith what God has already provided!" By understanding Dr. Stettler's teaching on who you are in Christ and the truth about your born-again spirit, you will revitalize your desire to live for Him. The practical aspect of Dr. Stettler's four-step Activation process will help your faith come alive, resulting in you becoming "doers of the word and not hearers only!" Finally, getting rid of the false identities that you have and putting on the true identity you have in Christ will become clearer as you go through the meditations at the end of the book.

Ronald Ovitt, Author, teacher, and President of *Empower Ministry*, Chicago, IL

Table Of Contents

Dedication ix
Forward xi
Introduction xiii

SECTION 1: THIRD HEAVEN PERSPECTIVE 1
    Chapter 1: How the Father Sees You 3
    Chapter 2: The Principle of the Upgrade 15
    Chapter 3: Catching Up with Your Spirit 22

SECTION 2: DISCERNING SOUL AND SPIRIT 27
    Chapter 4: Jesus in the Mirror 29
    Chapter 5: Perceiving The 'Real' You 37

SECTION 3: THE ACTIVATING PROCESS 41
    Chapter 6: The Activating Valve 44
    Chapter 7: The Activation Process 49
    Chapter 8: It's a Balancing Act 61

SECTION 4: YOUR TRUE IDENTITY 69
    Chapter 9: What's True About Your Born-Again Spirit 71
    Chapter 10: The Completeness of Forgiveness 80
    Chapter 11: The Gift of a Good Conscience 92
    Chapter 12: An Upgraded View of Repentance 98
    Chapter 13: Don't Get Hung by Your Tongue 102

SECTION 5: UPGRADING YOUR IDENTITY AT A DEEPER LEVEL 111
    Chapter 14: Recircuiting Your Mind 113
    Chapter 15: "Give Me Back My Stuff" 126
    Chapter 16: Taking Down Your Giants 139
    Chapter 17: A Soul that Prospers 148
    Chapter 18: Shortcuts to an Upgrade 155
    Chapter 19: An Upgrade of a Different Sort 161

SECTION 6: ACTIVATING PRAYERS 167
Chapter 20: Activating Your 'I Am Accepted' Profile. 169
Chapter 21: Activating Your 'I Am Secure' Profile 181
Chapter 22: Activating Your 'I Am Significant' Profile. 189

APPENDICES 195
Appendix A: You Are Accepted 195
Appendix B: You Are Secure 199
Appendix C: You are Significant 201
Appendix D: What You Have 203
Appendix E: What You Can Do 205
Appendix F: Answers to *Internalize & Apply* Questions 207
About the Authors. 215

Dedication

This book is dedicated first to our Lord Jesus Christ, Who through the ministry of the Holy Spirit, opened our eyes to my 'real' identity in Christ. This revelation of our identity, and how to activate that identity, has truly revolutionized both how we view the Lord and view ourselves. What a liberating and victorious way to live!

I, Lon, dedicate this book to my wonderful wife, Laurie, my companion, confidant, and friend. Her support and encouragement has been invaluable in the writing of this book. Her story is very much a part of the message of this book. Laurie graciously co-labors with me in the work of the ministry.

I, Laurie, thank you, Lon, for a lifetime of love, adventures, joy, encouragement, and family.

Forward

The chronic neurosis of our generation is a lack of self-worth. Whether it stems from a dysfunctional family history, the danger of comparison, or the listening of the wrong voices, it is based on a lie.

When you have a proper understanding of your worth to God, as the crown of His creation, and the price He paid for your salvation, it should radically change the way you think and behave as a believer.

Dr. Lon and Laurie Stettler's book, **Activating Your True Identity**, not only masterfully deals with who we are in Christ, but how to "renew your mind", to overcome every past lie from the enemy that robs you of your joy and effectiveness in His Kingdom.

Chapter 16, *Taking Down Your Giants*, was especially impactful for me. Lon adds different ways God upgrades your understanding of your identity in Christ. Even through the giants that everyone faces, God will use them in your life to take you to new levels of faith, as you see the goodness of God in every situation. Laurie's testimony is powerful!

I highly recommend this book as a powerful discipleship tool for every new believer, and every believer looking to deepen their faith as we see who we are in Christ Jesus.

Larry Burgbacher
Pastor of Faith Church (Summerville, SC) and
Assistant Superintendent of the South Carolina District
of the Assemblies of God

Introduction

There is a principle in Scripture that God makes the man before He makes the ministry. That is, God prepares or makes the man or the woman (their identity) before He makes and releases their ministry and assignments. God is the potter who upgrades one's personhood and character through circumstances that shape and mold them into a vessel He can use.

Moses, the deliverer, spent 40 years in the wilderness around Sinai where God was shaping Him to be the prepared leader for the children of Israel. Joseph, the dreamer, had to go through a prison experience for about 13 years to become the administrator full of wisdom, insight, and understanding to lead Egypt and save the children of Israel. God led Paul, the apostle, into the desert of Arabia for fourteen years to teach him and give him the revelation of God's plan for the Church.

All three of these leaders went through a wilderness experience. We had our own wilderness experience that the Lord used to upgrade us and later to release us into ministry and to write this book.

Laurie speaking:

In August of 2015, I was driving up the interstate from Cincinnati to Columbus, Ohio, to have lunch with friends and then babysit our granddaughter. As I was driving north, a trailer being pulled by a pickup truck from the opposite direction became disconnected from the truck and proceeded as a projectile across the median and hit my SUV in a driver-side overlap crash. This drove my vehicle into the ravine next to the highway where it stopped, facing the highway.

My left femur was broken as was the C2 bone in my neck. I was taken by helicopter to a trauma hospital in Kettering, Ohio where I underwent surgery for both broken bones. I spent three weeks on the rehab floor of the hospital with Lon driving up from Cincinnati after work each day to visit.

Once released from the hospital, I could not return home because our house was a tri-level home not suitable for a wheelchair. We were blessed to live in an available one-story home belonging to friends for four months until I could return to our own home.

But there was more bad news: We learned at the follow-up visit to the orthopaedic surgeon that the X-ray showed an additional fracture that would require another surgery on my injured leg. The surgeon had to remove the rod from the first surgery and replace it with a shorter rod in my left femur. Multiple screws and other hardware were needed to stabilize the broken bone. It required 67 staples to put my leg back together (Lon counted!).

We continued living in our friend's home until I progressed from wheelchair to crutches. During this time, our only daughter was getting married in Charleston, South Carolina. We drove from Cincinnati to Charleston over two days to get to the venue. Lon took me, the mother of the bride, down the aisle in a wheelchair for the outdoor wedding and reception.

After four months of living at this alternative house, I was able to return to our home. I was a high school ESL teacher and missed the first three quarters of the school year before returning to work full-time for the fourth quarter.

During this process, we had a decision to make: Were we going to let this accident make us bitter or make us better? We decided to use this situation to make us better. We quickly drew near to the Lord during this time in our wilderness. The Lord led us to focus on who He is and who we are in Him. "*I am a victor, and not a victim*" quickly became our living motto (I Cor. 15:57). We wanted no pity because the Lord was developing His special treasure in each of us. Jesus came alive within us and became our treasure.

God used this wilderness time to upgrade both of us in our identity in Him. First, He upgraded us in our standing in Him as we learned about our identity in Christ. He daily upgraded us in "who we were becoming." We were discovering the sovereignty, majesty, and supremacy of Jesus in everything. God was strengthening our standing in Him.

We took this upgraded identity and standing into our situation to fully be the victor and not the victim. We received the spiritual resources we needed to overcome and be the head and not the tail in this season.

Introduction

Returning to the principle that God makes and equips the person before releasing the ministry and related assignments, we have now launched into the ministry the Lord has for us. (Lon's calling is to the office of teacher and author and Laurie's calling is to serving and mercy.)

Writing a book was not on the bucket list for either of us but was an assignment from the Lord that Lon received through a prophetic word in August of 2019. In January of 2020, the infamous COVID year, the Lord prompted him that this was the time to write it. This book is the second edition of the book from that initial assignment.

What you will discover in the pages which follow is what we both learned during this journey. We learned about who God is, how He views us as His heirs, and how we are to view ourselves. As you read through the pages, it is our prayer that you will discover how the Father sees you and apply the processes we share to activate your true identity.

Section 1:

A Third Heaven Perspective

Where does our story begin? It begins with our Father in heaven who is seated on the throne, ruling and reigning in the third heaven. So does your story.

In eternity past each of us existed and lived in the Father. Then, as now, we lived, and moved, and had our being in the Father. We frolicked in the glory of heaven as a spirit being. Before we were conceived in our mother's womb, the Father knew us and before we were born, He ordained our days and our future. The Father, the prolific writer that He is, wrote a complete destiny book for each of us before we were conceived and born. He wrote our purpose and good plans He had for us (Acts 17:26; Jer. 1:5; Ps. 139:16).

There was a day in eternity past when the members of the Godhead sat down and decided who they created you to be. They determined why you would come to earth and what your purpose would be. So before you were born, the Father wrote your thesis, your purpose. His plan contains all the good things He planned for you — to give you a future and a hope (Jer. 29:11). The Father was pretty excited about this plan!

God has a great plan for every one of us. Your future is bright and your destiny is good; there are no disasters planned by God for your life. The enemy may have some planned, but God and His kingdom do not. His plans are only good and they are designed to give you a bright future filled with hope. The Father is absolutely good. He weaves all of our circumstances together in such a way that continually upgrades our hearts to fulfill that great plan.

The fall of Adam and Eve into sin caused our innocent nature to become defaced and it needed to be re-created once again. The Father in His wisdom sent His only beloved son, Jesus, to die on the cross for us to pay for our sins and remove that defaced sin nature we inherited from Adam.

Through the finished work of Jesus, the Father gave us the nature of Christ, created in righteousness and true holiness. He positionally co-seated us in Christ at His right hand in the third heaven. The Father placed us in Christ so He could treat us just like He treats Jesus! You are a third heaven creation, who receives third heaven revelation, and you walk in third heaven authority.

Holy Spirit weaves together all of the life circumstances that we each experience so we will fulfill His great plan and purpose.

This is where we will pick up our story – with how our Father and all of heaven view us in the third heaven. Laurie and I invite you into our story and desire it to be your story as well.

Chapter 1

How The Father Sees You

I have redeemed you; I have called you by name; you are Mine! (Isaiah 43:1)

Have you ever wondered:

*How does the Father **see** or view me? Jesus view me? Holy Spirit view me?*
*What do they **think** of me?*
*How do they **talk** to one another about me?*
*How do the angels and host of heaven **talk** about me?*

We all have perceptions about others, and some of those perceptions are correct and others are not. How you perceive another person is a lens or filter that you use to view them over time.

The sequence works like this:

Your perception ⟶ Your thinking + attitude ⟶ Your speaking (words)

Your **perception** impacts what you **think** is true, which in turn impacts your **words** – how and what you speak.

- You have perceptions of how you view each member of the Godhead.
- You have perceptions about yourself.
- And you have perceptions about how you think the Father, Jesus, and Holy Spirit view you.

As you learn more about another person or about a member of the Godhead, your perception of them gets updated. Likewise, as you learn more about yourself, looking into the mirror of God's word, you will learn more not only about how God sees you, but be upgraded in your view or perception of yourself.

As you learn to perceive yourself the way the members of the Godhead see you, you will better align with the Father in your thinking and your words about yourself. And you will think and talk about your destiny in an upgraded way.

Let's Ponder!

What if your perception of God – who and how He is – isn't completely accurate?

What if your perception of how God sees you is inaccurate?

And, what if your perception of yourself as a child of God is not completely accurate?

One Version of You

Once you are born-again, the Godhead only sees you as a new person. You have the image of the Son. Jesus put a full layer of Himself — His personhood and deity — into you when you were born-again. You now have a born-again spirit. That is what They see every day and in every situation. They are calling you up into your real identity in Christ as a beloved son or daughter.

The Godhead does not have two views of you.

> There is only one version of you – your new man.

The Father, the Son, and Holy Spirit do not see two versions of you – the old man and the new man. They do not have double vision. There is only one version of you – your new man — living in Jesus and learning to be one with Him. The Godhead is not double-minded about you.

The Father sees you in Jesus. Your quality of life in Him is the same as what the Father enjoys with Jesus and Holy Spirit. You are a new creation walking in First Love with your God, and learning how to live in the secret place of Christ within. The Father loves you the way He loves Jesus. He sees Jesus in you. The Holy Spirit, your Helper, loves you the same way He loves the Father and Jesus.

When Jesus the Son died, so did you. He died <u>for</u> you and He died <u>as</u> you.

Did He die as you? Yes.

When He died, did you die also on the Cross? Yes.

When He was buried, who was buried with Him? The old you!

When He rose again to newness of life, who also rose with Him? You! His life, righteousness, grace, holiness, faith, character, and power all belong to you now in Jesus!

The Father now only speaks to you in your identity as a *saint*, never as a *sinner*. The Godhead only works on the new you. The old you is dead so leave it alone.

> **The Father only speaks to you in your identity as a *saint*, never as a *sinner*.**

Before you were born, the Father sat down and wrote your entire destiny book – why He created you.

> *I am fearfully and wonderfully made. . .In Your book were all written the days that were ordained for me.* Psalm 139:14, 16

Your destiny is in the DNA of your identity as a saint. When the Father looks at you, He sees your identity with the destiny (or purpose) that He had in mind when He created you for this time.

Everything about God is marvelous! He is saying, "I'm marvelous. I'm going to teach you to walk with Me so that everybody else will think you are marvelous as well."

You need a lifestyle that is absolutely dependent on majesty. You have access to a lifestyle that is marvelous and majestic, and which contains the sovereignty and supremacy of Jesus. So *you can't be ordinary.*

Christ in you makes you a magnet for everything that is brilliant and extraordinary. With Christ in you, the glory of God is never far from your life and circumstances. All of heaven is attracted to Jesus who is in you.

> Christ in you makes you a magnet... All of heaven is attracted to Jesus who is in you.

Hear the Father's words to you:

Beloved, We are not seeing two of you...the old man and the new man. We do not have double vision. There is only one of you living in Jesus and learning to be one with Him. We are not in two minds (versions) about you. We only speak to your identity as a saint, never as a sinner. We only work on the new you. The old you is dead so let it rest in peace.

When Christ was raised from the dead, your old nature was left in the grave and was not resurrected.

When Jesus was buried, He took your old man with Him. When He was raised from the dead, He left your old nature behind in the grave. The old man was not resurrected. It is gone, finished forever. Your old man is dead. Christ died <u>for</u> you and <u>as</u> you.

The apostle Paul said this very clearly:

> *Therefore if anyone is in Christ, he is a new creature; the old things* [old man] *passed away; behold, new things have come. Now all these things are from God.* (2 Corinthians 5:17-18a, bracket added)

> God only deals with the new man in us, because Jesus killed off the old man on the cross.

The old man was crucified and buried with Christ and the new man was raised to newness of life.

The Father only sees one version of you. He sees you only in Christ. God only deals with the new man in us, because Jesus killed off the old man on the cross.

Old Self: Rom. 6:6; Col. 3:9; Eph. 4:22   **New Self:** Col. 3:10; Eph. 4:24

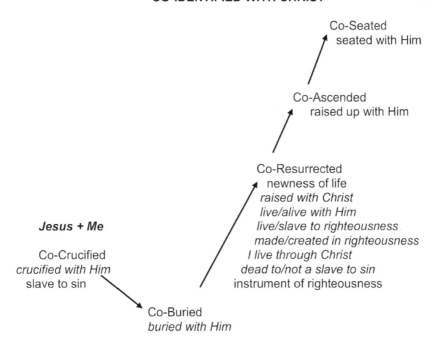

Co-Identified with Christ

Here are the scriptural references for your further study:

Co-Crucified: Galatians. 2:20; Romans 6:6

Co-Buried: Romans 6:4; Colossians 2:12

Co-Resurrected: Romans 6:4, 8, 11; 1 Peter 2:24; Colossians 2:13; Ephesians 2:4-5; 2 Corinthians 5:21; Ephesians 4:24

Co-Ascended: Ephesians 2:4-6; Colossians 3:1

Co-Seated: Ephesians 2:6

In summary, when Jesus Christ rose from the dead in newness of Life, none of your old nature made it through the resurrection. It was left behind in the grave. Now the Father only sees the new you in Jesus. The old you is dead.

> **None of your old nature made it through the resurrection. It was left behind in the grave.**

Listen to the Father's words to you:

When My beloved Son rose from the dead in newness of Life none of your old nature made it through the resurrection. The old you is dead. It was left behind. We made sure of it.

When My Son died, so did you. He died for you and He died as you.

When He was buried, He took your old man with Him. When He was raised from the dead, He left your old nature behind. The old man can never be resurrected. It is gone, finished forever.

Your new man is Christ in you, giving you His nature.

When Christ died for you, He killed off the old man because it was not modifiable.

Why did the Father kill off the old man? Because He didn't want the bother of changing your old nature. Our Father didn't want the hassle of changing the old you using *behavior modification*. He already showed us that this does not work with the children of Israel consistently failing to modify their behavior to keep the Law. Your old nature was not modifiable.

> **The Father put you in Christ, and Christ into you, so He could treat you like He treats Jesus.**

Instead, the Father wanted to give you an entirely new man or race (*anthropos*) that has never existed before —the nature of Christ that is magnificent, majestic, supreme, and glorious (Eph. 2:15)! The Father put you in Christ, and Christ into you, so He could treat you like He treats Jesus. You stand today before God as if you were Christ, because Christ stood before God as if he were you. You are a 3rd heaven creation, who receives 3rd heaven revelation, who has 3rd heaven authority (Eph. 2:6)!

You now have permission to consider yourself dead to sin and alive unto Him. That is how the Father sees you.

Consider yourself to be dead to sin, but alive to God in Christ Jesus. Romans 6:11

Why should you consider yourself dead to sin? Because the Father does.

He will teach you the lifestyle of being alive in Him. So when God looks at you, He doesn't see anything wrong, because He killed off all sin and negativity. He's really happy about that now. He is not dealing with your sin because He already dealt with it once and for all (Rom. 6:10; Heb. 7:27; I Pet. 3:18). God does not and has not charged sin to any believer's account for over 2,000 years!

You are no longer a slave to sin. It is no longer your nature. The old nature is dead and at rest in the grave. God does not have a *sin conscious* view of you, because Jesus dealt with sin once and for all. Rather, the Godhead has a *righteousness conscious* view of you made in Their image and likeness.

Most of us have been resurrecting our old nature for so long that we qualify as apostles. We are raising the dead every single day. We raise more corpses from the dead than all the apostles combined! We unknowingly resurrect our old nature – a dead corpse — by default.

You may find yourself asking:

> "I seem to always *default* to the old man rather than my new nature. I unknowingly respond from the flesh rather than from the Spirit. I'm learning Jesus killed off my old man at the cross and left it in the grave. How do I stop going directly to the old man and instead live only in my new nature?

Here's the thing: Even though your old nature was positionally co-crucified and co-buried with Jesus, your old nature is still present in you. Your flesh nature will default to it and resurrect it . . . if you allow it. Consider yourself dead to sin and alive unto Him. Don't work on your sin; work on your righteousness, your true identity. That's what the Father is doing: upgrading your identity, not your sin.

Let's apply Luke 9:23-24 to what we are learning:

> *"If anyone wishes to come after Me, he must deny himself* [old nature], *and take up his cross daily and follow Me. For whoever wishes to save his life* [old nature] *will lose it, but whoever loses his life* [old nature] *for My sake, he is the one who will save it.* (brackets added)

Deny your old nature, do not default to it; rather, consider yourself dead to it and live free in Christ. Surrender your will to His will. Ask Jesus to fill you with the Holy Spirit so you display the fruit of the Spirit. Christ came to free you from the trappings of the old nature, so stay free in Christ!

As we continue through this book, you will learn several ways to put off the old man so you can return to the new man. For now, please know your new man is Christ in you, giving you His nature. Your new man has all the things required to walk with God. It is built into Jesus who is in you.

God is not practicing behavior modification on your old man in an attempt to upgrade your old nature. But religion is.

Religion is about trying to change the behavior of your old nature. But God is not practicing behavior modification on you. He is not upgrading your old nature. He already killed off your old man and placed it in the grave. Behavior modification does not work on a dead corpse.

> God is not calling out your behavior. He is calling you up into your identity.

God gave you a new Christ nature and now reprograms your mind with the mind of Christ and your will to reflect the ways of the new man rather than resort to habits of the old man. You do not become a new person by changing your behavior. You became the new man when you received Christ into your spirit.

God is not calling out your behavior, He is calling you up into your identity.

How You are Known in Heaven

God is always speaking to you from your true identity in Him.

How you are known in heaven is your persona and all life circumstances must line up with it. Since you are in Christ at the Father's right hand, so are all your circumstances.

God is always speaking to you from your true identity in Christ. The three persons of the Godhead are working with you to overcome negativity and wrong perceptions about yourself.

> **Since you are in Christ at the Father's right hand, so are all your circumstances.**

Let's Ponder!

What would be an upgrade for you in terms of your perspective and language (words), in how you view yourself?

God is upgrading your persona with *encounters* and with *processes* so you will perceive, think, and talk about yourself the way that heaven does. Sometimes He first gives you the encounter with Him, and then the process. Other times, He allows a situation to occur and you learn the process through encounters with Him.

We need to love the learning in order to prosper. Encounters and processes target and expose who you are in order to upgrade your identity in Him.

You overcome wrong perceptions and negativity by stepping into your identity: your persona or how you are known in heaven.

Declaration: I declare that I will step into my identity in Christ and overcome wrong perceptions and negativity about myself.

The three persons of the Godhead planned your long-term future by giving personal scriptures, prophetic words, dreams and visions so that you know:

- who They want you to become in Christ
- the role They want you to have in the Kingdom
- the gifts that are available to you every day in your life in Them

God see you as a learner, not a failure, not a loser. Anything less would be an insult to the finished work of Christ.

The three persons of the Godhead are constantly upgrading Their presence in you. They are elevating you in Their presence so that you are empowered to receive every gift that is yours already in Christ.

It is important that you live in God's declarations about you, that you constantly confess His declarations over you. The New Testament idea of *confess* simply means "to agree and say what God says."

Let's Ponder!

1. Do you believe what the Father believes and says about you?

2. Can you see yourself as powerful in Jesus? Do you have impossible situations? How about letting Him into these situations? He has endless possibilities!

3. The Father is delighted to give to you. Are you as excited to receive as He is to give?

4. Jesus and the Holy Spirit are constantly praying to the Father on our behalf. Did you know you can join them in their conversation?

Let's Internalize and Apply!

1. The Father only has one view of you. What is that view?

   _____

   _____

   _____

2. Where is your old nature now?

   _____

   _____

   _____

3. Why does God only deal with the new man in us?

   _____

   _____

   _____

4. The Father put you in Christ, and Christ in you, so that He could treat you like whom?

   _____

   _____

   _____

5. What happens in your life when you default to your old nature instead of the new man?

_____

_____

_____

6. Why is the Godhead not practicing behavior modification on you?

_____

_____

_____

7. T/F – God is always speaking to you from your identity in Christ. _____

Chapter 2

The Principle of the Upgrade

Be transformed [upgraded] *by the renewing of your mind. (*Romans 12:2, brackets added)

The Father is continually upgrading your identity in Christ. You need to know that your biggest battles are always about your true identity. These are assaults against your sonship in Christ and against the Christ living in you. Laurie's auto accident that nearly took her life was the setting of such a battle about identity for us.

Throughout our particular journey we learned a Scriptural principle, the *Principle of the Upgrade*. Each upgrade was needed to equip us with the spiritual resources we needed for our next assignment. The Principle of the Upgrade operated in three areas of our lives. We received:

> Your biggest battles are always about your true identity.

- greater revelation of our identity in Christ,
- greater revelation of who God is and what He is for us, and
- an increase in the growth and development of the fruit of the Spirit within us (Gal. 5:22-23).

We needed to be upgraded in these three areas as the weight and promise on our lives, and His destiny for us, was much bigger than we could handle staying where we were. The next season of our lives required a greater revelation of our identity in Christ and who and what He wanted to be for us. Additionally, we needed to manifest the fruit of the Spirit at a higher level. Thus, the *principle of the upgrade*.

We discovered that the more we learn about our true identity in Christ and the fruit of the Spirit He's upgrading in us, the more we learn about Jesus and the Father. And the more we learn about God, the more we learn about who we really are.

The upgrading process can be likened to an upward spiral. One of the definitions of spiral in Merriam-Webster's dictionary is "the advancement to higher levels through a series of cyclical movements."[1]

The core definition of spiral is the continual moving up to higher levels. The Father is spiraling you to higher levels in your identity, so look up and move up. By looking upwards and keeping your gaze on Him, you are moving up in your walk in Him with greater trust, stronger faith, and an expectant heart.

Sometimes the rate of the upgrading spiral increases and at other times it decreases. Once an upgrade to your identity is firmly established in you, the Father will say, "you are finished on this level, so come up higher. It's time to move up to the next level." Your identity in six months should be higher than it is today.

Let's Ponder!

What revelation of your identity in Christ is the Lord desiring to upgrade in you?

What revelation of who God is or what He is for you is the Lord seeking to upgrade in you?

What fruit of the Spirit is the Lord seeking to grow and develop in you today?

Upgrading Your Identity

Holy Spirit brings revelations of truths from Scripture about your identity. Remember, perception is your filter or lens. Identity truths from Scripture will give you an accurate **perception** of your identity, leading to you accurately **think** about yourself. For example, if you genuinely think: "I

---

[1] "Spiral." Merriam-Webster.com Dictionary, Merriam-Webster, https://www.merriam-webster.com/dictionary/spiral. Accessed 7 Nov. 2022.

am the righteousness of God in Christ Jesus," then your **spoken** words about yourself will make a positive impact in the natural and spiritual realms. The result will be an **upgraded view** of your identity in Christ that aligns with God's singular version of you as a righteous son or daughter.

Take a look at this illustration:

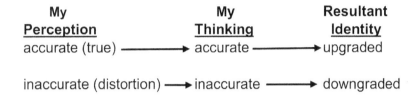

God is inviting you to VIEW yourself, THINK about yourself, and TALK about yourself the same way that heaven does. You cannot afford to think thoughts about yourself that God has not thought about you.

Laurie speaking: *This dynamic is what we had to learn through our wilderness experience. Our believing, thinking, and speaking out our living motto "I am a victor, not a victim" was key to seeing ourselves in an upgraded way (I Cor. 15:57). We were also experiencing an upgrade in seeing ourselves as overcomers (I Jn. 5:4) and more than conquerors (Rom. 8:37).*

*The fruit of the Spirit that was developed in me during this season was that of **patience** and **joy**. James 1:2-4 tells us that the testing of our faith produces endurance that makes us complete (can I say upgraded). Endurance was an area that was being developed in me. In fact, my family made a plaque for my bedroom wall of this scripture from James highlighting the word "Endurance."*

*Lon speaking: In addition to our identity being upgraded, the Lord was also upgrading the development of the fruit of the Spirit in my life. This was a lesson in **humility** to learn to serve my wife in practical ways – folding and unfolding Laurie's wheelchair to go to places and appointments, fixing her meals, laundry, and the list goes on. We learned the fruit of **peace** that results in resting in the finished work of Christ. I believe the fruit that undergirded all of these was **self-control**. I had to be cool, calm, and collected and the organized one to make it through each day. I, of course, still have a lot of room to grow in each of these fruit.*

Our identity areas that were upgraded will be discussed as we progress through this book. A complete list of truths the Lord was upgrading in us are found in Appendices A through F at the conclusion of this book.

Your Identity Can Also Be Downgraded

There is an interesting example of being downgraded in Numbers 13 and 14 where Moses sent out 12 spies into the Promised Land. Upon their return, 10 of the spies saw themselves as grasshoppers (a diminished, downgraded view of their identity). Caleb, along with Joshua, came back with an upgraded identity than when they went out and saw themselves as powerful as the giants.

Like the 10 spies, if you accept inaccurate information about your identity, it ultimately results in a distorted, downgraded identity. The sequence looks like this:

- Labels people have put on you, lies of the enemy, what your mistakes say about you, or your own negative self-talk can give you an inaccurate **perception** of your identity, leading you to inaccurately **think** of yourself as less than a saint.

- Your **spoken** words about your identity negatively impact the natural and spiritual realms. This downgrades your **view** of your identity in Christ – resulting in a counterfeit and distorted view.

Upgrading Who God is For You

Coupled with the upgrading process in our identity and fruit of the Spirit, we also began to gain an elevated perception of who God was for us. What we think about God – who and what He is – is the most important thing about us. In our times with the Lord, Holy Spirit brought revelation from Scripture as to who the members of the Godhead were for us.

Here are some things we learned:

- Truths from the scriptures of who God is gave us an accurate **perception** of Their nature, which changed our **thinking** about each member of the Godhead

- Our **spoken** words about the Lord made a positive impact on our lives and in the spiritual realm

- We began to see an **upgraded view** of who the Lord is for us. We began to see the Father as more loving, more gracious, and a present help.

This is shown in the illustration below.

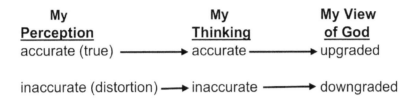

Laurie and Lon speaking: *What we learned about who God is and what He was for us was huge! Our loving heavenly Father is absolutely good. He was our provider and coach. Jesus redeemed our circumstance and was the healer and restorer of Laurie's body. Holy Spirit was our counselor, comforter, encourager, and friend. We received an abundance of grace, mercy and kindness from the Lord.*

A Distorted View of God

As you noticed in the above illustration, your view of God will be distorted if you accept inaccurate information about the Lord.

- Statements from religion, from the world system, or from the enemy (the devil) all give you an inaccurate **perception** of who God really is, leading you to **think** about the Lord in an inaccurate way. For example, you may inaccurately perceive that God does not care about you, which affects your thinking and the words you say.

- Your **spoken** words have a negative impact on you and express doubt and unbelief toward who God really is for you. This downgrades and distorts your **view** of who God is for you. As a result, you might see Him as less loving or caring, less trustworthy, not interested in you, or even harsh.

The more you learn about your true identity in Christ, the more you learn about Jesus and the Father. And the more you learn about God, the more you learn about who you really are.

Principle of the Upgrade in Scripture

The Scripture is replete with examples of the Principle of the Upgrade in operation. Here are several examples which are instructive. We already learned about how the 10 spies saw themselves as grasshoppers (a diminished, downgraded view of their identity) while Caleb and Joshua came back with an upgraded identity.

David was upgraded from a shepherd to a warrior king. His revelation of God was also upgraded to seeing God as the Lord of Hosts, the God of angel armies. David discerned that he had heaven's assistance in the battle. (1 Samuel 17)

Gideon was upgraded in his identity as a valiant warrior who went forth using the Lord's strategy to defeat the Midianites. His revelation of God was upgraded to see God as Jehovah Shalom, the God our Peace. (Judges 6)

Moses was upgraded to be a deliverer and prophet to lead the children of Israel out of Egypt. He received the revelation of God as I AM WHO I AM. (Exodus 3 & 4)

Jacob's name (supplanter) was upgraded to **Israel** (one who contends). His revelation of God was upgraded to seeing Him as God Almighty. (Genesis 32 & 35)

Abram's name (exalted father) was upgraded to **Abraham** (father of a multitude) while Sarai's name (barren one) was upgraded to **Sarah** (princess). Their revelation of God was upgraded to God Almighty as covenant maker and covenant keeper. (Genesis 17)

Saul became **Paul** when he was upgraded from a persecutor of the church to an apostle and advocate for the church. His revelation of God was upgraded when He received a personal revelation of Jesus as the Christ on the way to Damascus. (Acts 9)

God is using this same principle today to upgrade you to fulfill His destiny for your life. Your responsibility is to cooperate with Him.

Let's Internalize and Apply!

1. What three areas does God upgrade in your life through each circumstance He takes you through?

   _____

   _____

   _____

2. Each upgrade in you can be likened to an upward spiral. What does this mean?

   _____

   _____

   _____

3. What does an upgraded view of your identity align you with?

   _____

   _____

   _____

4. What are the sources which might give you a distorted or downgraded view of who and what God is for you?

   _____

   _____

   _____

Chapter 3

Catching Up with Your Spirit

> *For we are His workmanship* [masterpiece], *created in Christ Jesus.*
> (Ephesians 2:10a, bracket added)

It has been said that *art* – such as music, a sculpture, a painting — represents the *artist*. If you want to know an artist, simply study their work and you will gain understanding of the artist.

God is the ultimate and greatest of all artists. The crowning jewel of God's creation is you! You are His masterpiece! This is what we will be learning in this book – learning about the art (you) and the Artist (God).

If you want to see the *best-of-the-best* of all God has made in the universe, you don't need a telescope or a microscope. What you need is a *mirror*. More specifically, a *spiritual mirror*!

The Scripture — God's Word – is our spiritual mirror. Let's begin to see God's perspective. The first step is to look closely in God's mirror!

In the first chapter of the book of James, the writer makes reference to two different mirrors. In verse 23, James refers to a physical mirror like the bathroom mirror you probably looked into this morning:

> *For if anyone is a hearer of the word and not a doer, he is like a man who looks at his natural face in a **mirror**...*

Then in verse 25, he refers to a *spiritual* mirror, which is God's Word:

> *But one who looks intently at the perfect law, the law of liberty* [God's Word – specifically the New Testament], *and abides by it, not having become a forgetful hearer but an effectual doer, this man will be blessed in what he does.* (bracket added)

Now, God's Word as a spiritual mirror addresses every facet of our lives, but for our purpose *God's Word perfectly reflects who you are in your born-again spirit*. "Therefore if anyone is in Christ, he is a new creature; the old things passed away; behold, new things have come" (2 Cor. 5:17). God's Word as a spiritual mirror is reflecting perfectly who you are in your born-again spirit.

Have you ever read God's Word, specifically the New Testament, and wondered if the writer is talking about your born-again spirit or your soul? I have. Then, I started asking the Holy Spirit (Who moved upon men to write the Scriptures) to help me discern whether the author was speaking about my born-again spirit or my soul. It made all the difference in the world!

Lon speaking: *I remember a small group leader asking me: "Are you holy?" And, "Are you righteous?" At that time, I responded something like, "I try to live a holy life." or "I try to be righteous." Over time, I learned that I lacked understanding of the relationship between my spirit and soul. I seemed to mesh the two together. I was mixing up what Christ did and what I do. I now know that I am holy and righteous in my born-again spirit as a result of the finished work of Christ. My responsibility now is to live out what has already transpired in my born-again spirit – live out holiness.*

As we begin, we invite you to reach for your Bible and hold it in your hands and make this declaration with me:

> "This is my Bible. I am who it says <u>I am</u>. I have what it says <u>I have</u>. And I <u>can do</u> what it says I can do."

Your born-again spirit accurately reflects who you *are*, what you *have* in Christ, and what you *can do* through Him.

Let's look into the spiritual mirror again at another verse in the New Testament that refers to a *spiritual mirror*.

> *But we all, with unveiled face, beholding as in a mirror* [God's Word] *the glory of the Lord* [reflecting the glory of your born-again spirit], *are being transformed*

[in your soul] *into the same image* [found in your born-again spirit] *from glory to glory. . .* (2 Corinthians 3:18, brackets added)

Notice this verse is *not* speaking of our born-again spirit that is being transformed, as our spirit being was completely transformed when we were born-again. Rather, this verse is talking about our *soul* that is being transformed.

> **Your soul needs to catch up with what has already transpired in your born-again spirit.**

As you gaze into God's spiritual mirror, His Word, your soul begins to see with spiritual eyes and become transformed to what is in your born-again spirit. Your soul needs to catch up with what has already transpired in your born-again spirit. That is, your soul is being upgraded to what is true in your spirit. Your soul is what is being transformed!

Paul said to the Galatians:

My children [Galatian believers], *with whom I am again in labor until Christ* [in your born-again spirit] *is formed in you* [your soul and heart]. (Galatians 4:19, brackets added)

Likewise, Paul said to the Philippians:

. . .work out [activate into your soul] *your salvation* [from your born-again spirit] *with fear and trembling.* (Philippians 2:12, brackets added)

Paul was saying that what is true about your born-again spirit does *not* automatically become active and operational in your soul; these truths must be implanted or activated. He labored with the Galatians, the Philippians and all the churches to activate the believers' identity in Christ, so their soul would catch up to their born-again spirit. The process of activation must be intentional and deliberate on the part of the believer.

> **What is true about your born-again spirit does *not* automatically become active and operational in your soul; these truths must be implanted or activated.**

Let's first learn about the 'real' you that God created you to be in your born-again spirit, and then how your soul becomes transformed.

Let's Internalize and Apply!

1. To see the best-of-the-best of all God has made in the universe, you need a spiritual mirror. What is your spiritual mirror?

   _____

   _____

   _____

2. What is meant by the statement, "Your soul needs to catch up with what has already transpired in your born-again spirit?"

   _____

   _____

   _____

3. T/F–What is true about your born-again spirit does not automatically become active and operational in your soul; these truths must be implanted or activated. _____

Section 2:

Discerning Soul And Spirit

For the word of God is living and active and sharper than any two-edged sword, and piercing as far as the division of <u>soul</u> and <u>spirit,</u> of both joints and marrow, and able to judge the thoughts and intentions of the heart.
(Hebrews 4:12, underline added)

The writer of the book of Hebrews and the Apostle Paul clearly understood the distinction between soul and spirit. Paul told the Thessalonian believers, "may your *spirit*, and *soul* and body be preserved complete, without blame at the coming of our Lord Jesus Christ" (I Thess. 5:23).

To a great extent, the Christian life consists of your soul catching up – being upgraded — with what has already transpired in your born-again spirit as you move toward full personhood – from glory to glory. Your mind and heart are being "transformed by the renewing your mind" (Romans 12:2). As a result of implanting the Word in your soul, your soul becomes conformed to the image of Christ (Rom. 8:29). *The end goal of the activation process is to move you from a 'sin-consciousness' view of yourself to developing the gold standard, a 'righteousness consciousness.'*

Chapter 4

Jesus in the Mirror

You were created to look and be like God. The Psalmist said you are "fearfully and wonderfully made."

> *Then God said, 'Let Us make man in Our image, according to Our likeness. . . God created man in His own image.* Genesis 1:26–27

> *. . .I am fearfully* [to stand in awe of] *and wonderfully made.* (Psalm 139:14b, brackets added)

We are *amazing*.

We are *completely amazing* and *awesome*, and we can prove it.

Now let us say something about you: You are more *awesome* and *wonderful* than you know.

Can you picture it? The Creator of the universe, who created you, takes a couple of steps back and looks at you and says, "Wow, you are awesome!" He stands in awe of you, His creation.

God *created* us, and now *recreated* us (you are now a 'new creation'), in such a way that we provide an accurate reflection of His glory back to Him and onto the world.

We invite you to look in God's mirror to see what He sees. You will look a whole lot like Jesus!

Each one of us is unique, and we were created to provide the most complete mirror image of God on earth. We reflect "Jesus in the Mirror!"

Identity Formation

Miles McPherson points out that we have two competing mirrors that we look at that affect our identity formation on the inside. There is a right mirror and a wrong mirror to view.[2]

The Right Mirror, God's Word. As a believer in Jesus, you now have an *I AM factor* from God – your individual uniqueness – which positions you above all living things to be in relationship with God. You look into your spiritual mirror, God's Word, to see who you are in your born-again spirit which looks like Jesus — which Miles calls your *I AM factor*.

Your *I AM factor* reflects the *I AM-ness of God*, your 'God image'.

> *I am fearfully and wonderfully made.* Psalm 139:14
> *And You crown him with glory and majesty*! Psalm 8:5

Don't let anyone take your crown!

God has given you a new name – a "Christian". That new name reflects your I AM factor, the 'real you.' This new name has many facets which we will discover shortly.

Jesus, the Great I AM, has put His nature in our human spirit, and recreated our *I AM-ness*, the 'real me.'

The result is you will develop a 'righteousness consciousness' of yourself as you *own* the I Am-ness that you see in this spiritual mirror. You will see yourself as a *saint*, and not a *sinner*. A 'righteousness consciousness' is the gold standard you are to pursue.

The Wrong Mirror. The problem is we often have an inaccurate understanding of our new self as a Christian; we're not sure what is the 'real me'. Miles calls this inaccurate view our *I AM imposter*.

Your *I AM imposter* is an inaccurate or incomplete understanding of who you are as a Christian. It is a deception; a counterfeit version or knockoff of who God has created you to be.

Isaiah 55:8-9 captures this understanding.

---

[2] Miles McPherson, *God in the Mirror* (Grand Rapids, MI: Baker Publishing Group, 2013), 7-8, 13-32)

> *"For my thoughts are not your thoughts, Nor are your ways My ways," declares the Lord. "For as the heavens are higher than the earth, So are My ways higher than your ways and My thoughts than your thoughts."*

In the natural your thoughts (about you) are not God's thoughts about you. For God's thoughts about you and me are higher than our natural thoughts. You must look into God's spiritual mirror to see what God thinks about you – how God created you and sees you.

One way you develop this wrong understanding of yourself as a Christian is when you try to create a *name* for yourself separate from God – trying to create or find your significance, worth, and value, outside of God. Singer Frank Sinatra sang a song, *I Did It My Way*. Have you ever tried to create a name for yourself – apart from your relationship with God? How did that turn out?

Mistakes, Labels, and Lies

You are also looking in the wrong mirror when you think your identity is defined by the *mistakes* you've made, or the *labels* others have put on you, or the *lies* the Enemy has tried to put upon you. Together, these make up our I AM imposter.

Have you ever made a *mistake* like offended someone with your words; or yelled at your friend, spouse or child in anger; or did something disrespectful; or walked out on a relationship. A mistake is an event; it is not your *identity*! Refuse to be a prisoner of your past. Mistakes are a life lesson, not a life sentence.

Or perhaps you have believed the *labels* that others have spoken over you: you're just average; or inferior; not capable; have an addiction; or you're a loser.

> **A mistake is an event; it is not your identity!**

Maybe you have believed some of the *lies* the enemy has whispered in your ear, such as you don't have what it takes; you're not talented or special; you don't measure up.

And then there's the *negative self-talk* that doesn't let God get a Word in edgewise! If you don't silence those competing voices, they'll eventually deafen you. Which voice are you listening to?

A lie, a label, or a mistake can become the basis of the devil's accusation against you. Each of these are an assault against your sonship, your identity in Christ. However, when the enemy hears you assert your identity in Christ by rejecting those accusations, he no longer sees only you; he sees Jesus!

If you dwell on any of these too long, you begin to believe them and identify with them, and you think of them as your name. When this happens, they create a wrong mental image on the inside. If you're not careful, the wrong image (from labels, mistakes, lies, negative self-talk) will become deeply entrenched emotionally in your heart and very difficult to overcome. A name is a powerful thing.

If you think any of these are your identity, you are looking in the *wrong* mirror. Continuing to look in the wrong mirror will result in you seeing yourself as a sinner, having a *'sin consciousness'*.

As a Christian, you are NOT

- what your mistakes say you are
- the labels people put upon you
- the lies the Enemy says about you
- who you've tried to create yourself to be

> **Your actions or wrong thinking do not define your identity in Christ. What God has said about you, and provided through Jesus Christ, defines your identity.**

You *are who God says you are – deeply loved, completely forgiven, highly valued!*

What you may have done is <u>not</u> who you are. Your actions or wrong thinking do not define your identity in Christ. What God has said about you, and provided through Jesus Christ, defines your identity.

Let's Ponder!

What images do you have in your mind of who you are that are the result of looking in the wrong mirror – your mistakes?

Labels from others?

Lies of the enemy?

A name you've tried to create for yourself?

An Identity You Cannot Lose

Your God-given identity, which is in your born-again spirit, is something that you *cannot lose*. If something can be lost, then it is not your identity.

Too often we base our identity and self-worth on our:

- appearance
- talents and abilities
- smarts
- strength
- career success

But you can lose each one of these. Remember: *if you can lose it, it is not your real identity.*

Your God-given identity is based on *who God says you are* in the Bible, God's *spiritual mirror*, and not based on your appearance, or your talents/abilities, or your smarts, or your strength, or your successes.

You are who God says you are and you cannot lose it! The caveat is that you must live out the Christian life and ensure that you maintain your identify in Christ. Just as Adam and Eve forfeited their intimate relationship with God, so can you. Don't reject your great salvation resulting in your name being erased out of the Lamb's Book of Life (Rev. 3:5; Heb. 10:26, 29).

You were created to *wear the name* that you have been given – a name that reflects your I AM-ness from your Creator. Rather than make a name for yourself, wear the name that you have been given.

> *I have called you by name; you are Mine*! Isaiah 43:1

> *I will give him. . . a new name. . . I will write on him the name of My God. . .*
> Revelation 2:17; 3:12

Notice that God *exclusively* gets to name us, and not we ourselves or others (labels).

You not only bear God's image but you know His voice. Learning to hear the voice of God is key to discovering your destiny and fulfilling your potential. Know your true identity. When you know who you are, it doesn't matter who you are not. Don't focus on what you aren't, focus on what you are!

Is God's voice the *loudest* voice in your life?

That's the question.

If the answer is no, that's the problem.

Chronic noise may be the greatest impediment to your spiritual growth. When your life gets loud, with noise filling every frequency, you lose your sense of being. And when your schedule gets busy, you lose your sense of balance.

Pursue the truth about you which originates from your born-again spirit (which has access to the mind of Christ), and not from your natural mind. God's Word tells you what is true about your born-again spirit.

So where do you see yourself on the continuum below? Place an "X" on the continuum line below.

'I AM Factor' Continuum

I AM I AM

Imposter_____Factor

Let's trade in your *I AM imposter* for your true *I AM factor*! Run toward your God-given destiny rather than away from it! Wear the name you have been given!

> ## Let's Ponder!
>
> *How do you walk away from your "I AM imposter" so that you wear the name you've been given?*
>
> *What image do you see in the mirror? Which mirror are you looking at – I AM imposter? Your God image?*
>
> *How can you go from looking in the I AM imposter mirror (your mistakes, labels from others, lies from enemy) and flip the script so that you look more intently at your I AM factor – the 'real' you?*

In this book, we will be looking at your complete born-again-spirit portrait and will break it into smaller sub-profiles to help you better understand your born-again spirit. Once you understand each sub-profile, then you can *activate* each truth about your born-again spirit by revelation of the Holy Spirit and faith to help your soul catch up with what has already transpired in your born-again spirit.

Let's now take a closer look at who God says that we are – and look deeper into His mirror – God's Word — to see what God sees.

Let's Internalize and Apply!

1. What is meant by your "I AM factor"?

   _____

   _____

   _____

2. How does it differ from the "I AM imposter?"

   _____

   _____

   _____

3. How do you move from the "I AM imposter" to the "I AM factor?"

   _____

   _____

   _____

4. Have you ever tried to create a name for yourself – apart from your relationship with God — trying to find significance, worth, and value separate from God? How did that turn out? Who has the exclusive right to give you a name? How should you respond?

   _____

   _____

   _____

Chapter 5

Perceiving The 'Real' You

Now may the God of peace Himself sanctify you entirely; and may your <u>spirit</u> and <u>soul</u> and <u>body</u> be preserved complete, without blame at the coming of our Lord Jesus Christ. (1 Thessalonians 5:23, underline added)

Understanding Spirit, Soul, and Body

The Scripture says that we are a three-part being: spirit, soul, and body.

Spirit – Our innermost part.

Soul – Our mental, emotional part. Includes: mind, will, emotions, and conscience. Often called "personality."

Body – Our physical part.

You are a spirit, have a soul, and live in a body.

Our **body** has five senses, but those senses cannot directly discern what is in your born-again spirit.

That which is born of the flesh is flesh, and that which is born of the Spirit is spirit. (John 3:6)

Also, your **soul** (mind and emotions) cannot clearly discern what is in your born-again spirit.

God's Word is the only accurate way to perceive what is in your born-again spirit.

Looking into God's spiritual mirror is how you discern your born-again spirit. God's Word reveals spiritual reality about your born-again spirit – which is how God sees us as a reflection of Himself. He wants us to see ourselves the same way.

The words that I have spoken to you are spirit and are life. (John 6:63)

> God's Word is the accurate way to perceive the spirit realm. Looking into God's spiritual mirror is how you access your born-again spirit.

Understanding spirit, soul, and body unlocks the spirit realm so you can experience who you *are*, what you *have,* and *what you can do* in Christ. God's Word perfectly reflects who you are in your born-again spirit.

We learned previously that when the Godhead looks at you, they see only one version of you – your new nature in Christ. They only see you as a new creation in Christ in your born-again spirit. All of heaven sees your born-again spirit as the real you.

Each one of us is unique, and we were created to provide the most complete mirror image of God on earth. We see "Jesus in the Mirror!"

Let's Ponder!

What ways can you use God's mirror, His Word, to see yourself as the Heavenly Father sees you?

Every born-again believer has undergone a complete inner transformation.

> *Therefore if anyone* [you] *is in Christ, he is a new creature* [in your born-again spirit]; *the old things passed away* [from your spirit]; *behold, new things have come* [into your born-again spirit]. *Now all these things* [in your born-again spirit] *are from God* (2 Corinthians 5:17-18a, brackets added)

Your body and soul were not fully transformed when you were born again. The change occurred in your born-again spirit. The change in your spirit will have an immediate impact on your soul and your body – your whole person – resulting in a changed life!

> *. . .for you have been born again. . .through the living and enduring word of* God (I Peter 1:23)

The complete transformation of your body and soul won't be completed until you go to be with Jesus. At that time your soul will be completely transformed (I Cor. 13:9-10; 12) as well as your body (I Cor. 15:42-44; 52-53). The key point here is that this transformational change occurred in your born-again spirit, and looking into the Word of God (God's spiritual mirror) is the only way to perceive your spirit.

Let's Internalize and Apply!

1. What are the three parts of your being?

_____

_____

_____

2. Can you access your spirit in a natural way? Explain.

3. What is the only accurate way to perceive the spiritual realm?

4. What is meant by God's Word being a 'spiritual mirror'?

5. What transformation occurred when you were born again?

Section 3:

The Activating Process

L on speaking: *I still remember it like it was yesterday, the day that I was first introduced to the process of Activation. I didn't know that was what it was called or what it really meant. It was much later before I realized that the process of activation is how the kingdom of God works.*

It was a Sunday morning in August, and the worship service at the church I was attending to qualify to play on the church's softball team had just concluded. I had played softball for the church for two seasons and really felt at home at this church. The pastor, Roger, played on the softball team as well, and I had gotten to know him fairly well. I told him that I really liked the church and wanted to become a member. I wanted to belong and find my purpose.

Roger invited me to join him in the pastor's office. He pulled out a Bible and opened it to a passage that I have gotten to know quite well:

> *The word is near you, in your mouth and in your heart – that is, the word of faith which we are preaching [**hear** the Word], that if you confess with your mouth Jesus as Lord [**speak** the Word], and believe in your heart [**believe** the Word] that God raised Him from the dead, you will be saved; for with the heart a person believes, resulting in righteousness, and with the mouth he confesses, resulting in salvation [the **activation**]. . . faith comes from hearing, and hearing by the word of Christ. Rom. 10:8-10, 17 (brackets added)*

Roger talked me through the passage and asked if I had any questions. I asked a couple of clarifying questions that he answered. Then, Roger stepped away and asked that I continue to review these verses. Unbeknownst to me, he stepped out of his office and joined his wife and they began to pray that I would receive Christ as my Savior that day.

When Roger returned, he led me through the four steps of activation. I heard the Word that Roger spoke, and I believed in my heart that Jesus was Lord and that God raised Him from the dead. He then led me to confess with my mouth that Jesus is Lord and to repent of my sins, asking God to forgive me of all my sins. I then invited Jesus Christ into my heart to be my Savior and Lord. At that point, I felt an assurance that I was now a child of God—a result of salvation. That day I experienced the first application of the activation process in life.

In a general sense, *Activation* is the spiritual process of taking what is in the spiritual realm and bringing it into the natural so that it becomes active and operational in your life. In this current study, Activation is the process of bringing what is in your born-again spirit over into your soul – mind, will, and emotions — and into your life.

> *Stir up* [or activate] *the gift of God which is in you. . .* (2 Timothy 1:6, NKJV, brackets added)

> *Do not neglect* [or do not fail to activate] *the spiritual gift within you. . .* (I Timothy 4:14, brackets added)

The four steps identified in Romans 10:8-10 to activate the new birth (described in chapter 8 of this book) are the same steps to activate other important spiritual experiences of your life. The steps are the same but the context and applications are different. This is how the Kingdom of God operates.

The concept of *activation* applies in every area of the Christian life. The Activation spectrum is:

ACTIVATION
- to become born-again
- **to develop a righteousness consciousness**
- to manifest the fruit of the Spirit
- to receive the baptism in the Holy Spirit
- to manifest gifts of the Spirit

In this book, we are looking at the second application – developing a 'righteousness' consciousness (the gold standard!) – where you activate what has already transpired in your born-again spirit into your soul and the rest of your life!

As you may have experienced, what is true about you in the spiritual realm does *not* automatically become active and operational in your life; these truths must be activated. Your soul needs to catch up with what has already transpired and was provided in the Spirit. Remember, the end goal of activating what has transpired in your born-again spirit is to develop a righteousness consciousness in your mind and heart. This is how you are conformed to the image of Christ in your inner man (Rom. 8:29).

Chapter 6

The Activating Valve

Picture a *target* consisting of three circles inside each other.

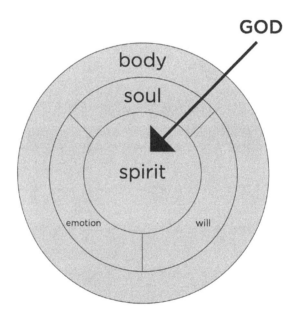

The outer circle is your *body*. It's the part you can see and feel.

The inner circle is your *soul*. It can't be seen but can be felt. Also, it touches both your body and your spirit.

The innermost circle is your *spirit*. Although it's the center of who you are, it can't be seen or felt. It's completely surrounded by your soul.

As we learned previously, your physical body has no direct access into your spirit.

Everything that comes out from your spirit to your body must go through your mental, emotional part. Your spirit is the core of your being, the "real you", your life-giving part.

Your soul acts as a valve[3] in between your spirit and your body, observes Andrew Wommack.

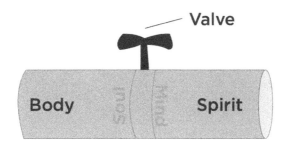

The Activating Valve

The flow of God's supernatural life from your spirit to your body (natural realm) depends on how open your soul is.

After being born again, the rest of your Christian life consists simply of *renewing* your mind (from God's spiritual mirror, His Word) and *releasing* what is in your born-again spirit.

As you renew your mind and believe God's Word, your soul will start to agree with what's already transpired in your spirit.

When your *spirit* and *soul agree* (keeping the 'flesh' at bay), you release and experience the life and peace of God. What's in your born-again spirit can now *flow through* your soul in order to get out to your body and into the rest of your life. You have a well of living water inside of you – in your born-again spirit. It's time to start taking and drinking of what you have already been given! This is being spiritually-minded.

---

[3] Andrew Wommack, *Spirit, Soul, & Body Study Guide* (Colorado Springs, CO: Andrew Wommack Ministries, Inc.), 2008

When your *body* and *soul agree* (often referred to as the 'flesh') separately from what is in your born-again spirit, you cut off the supernatural flow of life from your spirit. This is called being carnally-minded because you are walking like an unbeliever.

For the mind set on the flesh is death, but the mind set on the Spirit is life and peace. (Romans 8:6)

Your thinking can become dominated by:

- your mistakes
- labels from others
- lies of the enemy
- negative thoughts about yourself
- religion
- your senses

Your understanding becomes darkened, separating you from the life of God within. And this darkened understanding negatively affects you, your relationships, and your fellowship with God. You allow all this negativity to attach to your soul.

We have a natural inclination to look in the wrong mirror which results in wrong thinking and a wrong understanding of our identity. This occurs when a person is dominated by what they can see, taste, hear, smell, and feel instead of God's Word. They don't understand the change that happened in their born-again spirit or who they are in Christ. To them, something's just not "real" if it can't be perceived through their five natural senses. As a result, the flow of life from their born-again spirit stays turned off because they don't believe anything they can't see.

You need to develop a supernatural inclination to renew your mind and believe God's Word, so that your soul will start to agree with what has already transpired in your spirit.

The Christian life isn't a process of "getting from God"; it's a process of renewing your mind to perceive and releasing what you've already received. *You've already got it!* You have a well of living water inside of you – in your born-again spirit. It's time to start taking and drinking of what you have already been given!

It's much easier to release something you've already got than to go get something you don't yet have. Doubt is eliminated once you believe you've already got it!

Don't be conformed to this world, but be transformed by the renewing of your mind.

> *And do not be conformed to this world, but be transformed by the renewing of your mind, so that you may prove what the will of God is* [in your born-again spirit], *that which is good and acceptable and perfect.* **(Romans 12:2, brackets added)**

Your mind, thoughts, and attitudes determine whether you experience victory and the life of God in your spirit, or the defeat and death of the fallen natural realm.

It is *your* responsibility to renew your mind with the Word – God's spiritual mirror – and implant that truth into your soul and heart, resulting in transformation.

God's Word gives you the new values and attitudes you should conform yourself to. As you continually look into the Lord's spiritual mirror, you'll begin to see and experience yourself for who you really are.

Let's Internalize and Apply!

1. As a Christian, you are a born-again spirit, you have a soul, and you live in a body. So what is the 'real you'?

_____

_____

_____

2. When God the Father looks at you, what does He see?

_____

_____

_____

3. Now that you are born-again, your life consists of what two tasks?

_____

_____

_____

4. Now that you have a born-again spirit, what is the role of your soul?

_____

_____

_____

5. What does it mean when the scripture says you have "received his fullness"?

_____

_____

_____

Chapter 7

The Activating Process

Activating What God Has Appropriated

How do you transition your mind from looking at the wrong image (*I AM imposter*) to looking at your *I AM factor* image reflected in God's spiritual mirror? How does your soul catch up to what has already transpired in your born-again spirit?

You transform your soul (mind and heart) through the process of Activation.

Activation is that spiritual process of making what is in your born-again spirit become active and operational in your life. It is the process of activating what is in your born-again spirit and planting it into your soul – mind, will, and emotions.

What is true about your born-again spirit does *not* automatically become active and operational in your soul; these truths must be activated. Your *soul* needs to catch up with what has already transpired in your born-again spirit.

> **What is true about your born-again spirit does *not* automatically become active and operational in your soul; these truths must be activated.**

> *Stir up* [or activate] *the gift of God which is in you. . .* (2 Timothy 1:6, NKJV, brackets added)

> *Do not neglect* [or do not fail to activate] *the spiritual gift within you. . .* (I Timothy 4:14, brackets added)

What's in your born-again spirit must *flow into* your soul in order to get out to your body and into the rest of your life. Your soul acts as a 'valve' in between your spirit and your body.

The flow of God's supernatural life from your spirit to your body (natural realm) depends on how open your soul is. It is your responsibility to *form* the image of Christ in your born-again spirit into your soul and heart.

Activation turns the 'valve' all the way to *open*.

There are four steps (principles) involved in activation; the first three are the preparation and foundation, and the fourth is the actual act of activation.[4]

> *The word* [rhema] *is near you, in your mouth and in your heart – that is, the word* [rhema] *of faith which we are preaching* [**hear** the word], *that if you confess with your mouth Jesus as Lord* [**speak** the word], *and believe in your heart that God raised Him from the dead* [**believe** the word], *you will be saved; for with the heart a person believes, resulting in righteousness, and with the mouth he confesses, resulting in salvation* [the **activation**]. . . *faith comes from hearing, and hearing by the word* [rhema] *of Christ.* Rom. 10:8-10, 17 (brackets added)

> . . .*whoever says* [**speak** the word]. . . *and does not doubt in his heart, but believes that what he says is going to happen* [**believe** the word], *it will be granted* [**activated** to] *him. Therefore I say to you, all things for which you pray and ask, believe that you have received them, and they will be granted* [**activated**] *you.* Mark 11:23-24 (brackets added)

The Greek rhema means a "spoken word" from God.

Baseball Diamond. The four steps of biblical activation can be likened to the four bases of baseball. Getting to first base is *hearing* the word. Getting to second base is *believing* the word. Proceeding to third base is *speaking* the word. And finally, getting to home plate is *taking action* and activating the word to full operation. Unless a grace, truth, or a gift gets fully activated, it

---

[4] Bill Hamon, *Seventy Reasons for Speaking in Tongues* (Shippensburg, PA: Destiny Image Publishers, Inc., 2012), 119-124

does not count as crossing home plate – and is therefore unfruitful, dead, of no effect (James 1 and 2). So let us seek to bring each word that the Lord gives us to full activation in our life.

Four Steps of Activation

1. HEARING the Biblical Word of Truth on the Matter

All divine truths about your born-again spirit must be received by faith. Faith comes by **hearing God's word** or *rhema* of truth (Romans 10:17). You can then know the truth and the truth makes you free to believe and receive.

> *"The word is near you, in your mouth and in your heart" – that is, the word* [rhema] *of faith which we are preaching.* (Romans 10:8, bracket mine)

The Holy Spirit takes the written *Logos* Word and opens our spiritual eyes so the written word becomes a spoken and living *rhema* word.

What is in your born-again spirit is in *seed form* and must be activated and brought over to your soul. Hearing God's voice is a *seed* that you receive by revelation of the Holy Spirit and bring over into the natural realm.

Here are some of the ways that God personally speaks to you:

- The Holy Spirit causes a verse of Scripture to "leap off of the page" that is a truth or a promise to you personally
- You receive an idea or strategy that comes "out of the blue"
- You receive a prophetic word from another believer that is personally directed to you from God
- You have a prophetic dream in the night that the Lord is speaking to you
- You see a vision (snapshot or short video) from the Lord in the daytime when your eyes are open

These are all legitimate ways that you "hear" the word of the Lord to you personally. As you receive a word from the Lord, write it down! Keep a journal which you prayerfully revisit and speak forth in prayer.

When God gives you a word – a rhema, a prophetic word, a prophetic dream, or a vision – it means He trusts you to receive and faithfully carry that promise or word to full activation. If the Holy Spirit does not trust you to receive and carry the word or promise, then He would not give it to you. So spend time with the Lord and be receptive to the word He wants to plant in your heart today and carry it with faith and patience!

Words Have Assignments

Each word from the Lord has an *assignment* on it. This means that each word the Lord entrusts to you to carry to completion has an assignment on it. This applies to each rhema word, prophetic word, prophetic dream, and vision which the Lord gives to you.

> *So will the words that come out of my mouth not come back empty-handed. They'll do the work I sent them to do, they'll complete the **assignment** I gave them. (Isaiah 55:11 MSG)*

Any prophetic word or promise which God makes is impregnated with the seed of His life. When you receive the word from God, this begins the *conception phase*. God is saying, "My prophetic word to you will complete the assignment I give it if you will cooperate and partner with it to activate."

When you receive a word from the Lord, it assigns something to you that you must believe and decree, pray, and strategize-about with the Holy Spirit and take it to *the completion (full activation) phase*. You must live in that word, be fueled by it, steward it, grow it, and believe it. Don't abort it or let the passage of time rob you of God's promise or quench your faith. Don't let that word "fall to the ground."

Commit to make God's voice the loudest voice in your life.

   2. BELIEVING in the Heart

Romans 10:10 declares that "with the heart a person believes."

> *...out of the abundance of the heart the mouth speaks." (Matthew 12:34 NKJV)*

> *If you can believe, all things are possible to him who believes. (Mark 9:23 NKJV)*

Faith does not operate out of the head but from the heart. When faith is produced, it will operate only from the heart. From the truth, faith is born (formed) in the heart and becomes alive and active.

Faith comes into being when your spirit hears and believes the Word of God on the matter. Romans 10:8a says, "The word [of faith] is...in your heart."

Faith only functions within the heart of a person.

> Faith does not operate out of the head but from the heart.

People often have an understanding in their heart that is based on religion rather than the Bible. A wrong understanding of your identity that is deeply entrenched emotionally can be difficult to root out and replace with biblical truth.

When God gives you a word – be it a rhema word, a prophetic word, a prophetic dream, or a vision – He seldom gives you the *timeline*. Recall that when God gave a promise to the patriarchs in the Old Testament, He did not give them a timeline. Abraham believed for 25 years for the promised son Isaac; David waited 20 years to be fully installed as Israel's king; and Joseph waited 22 years to see the fulfillment of God's promises.

And some of the promises to patriarchs were fulfilled after they died. For example, Abraham's descendants did not take possession of the land promised to Abraham until over 400 years after the promise was made to him (Gen. 15:13).

So what do we do between the conception phase and the completion or activation phase of the word of the Lord to us?

> *For you have need of endurance* [to remain under the promise], *so that when you have done the will of God, you may receive what was promised.* (Hebrews 10:36, bracket and underline added)

> *Be...imitators of those who through faith and patience inherit the promises.* (Hebrews 6:12, underline added)

> *With respect to the promise of God, he* [Abraham] *did not waver* [stagger, vacillate, go back-and-forth] *in unbelief but grew strong in faith, giving glory to God. (Rom. 4:20, brackets added)*

Since God typically does not give us a timeline, our response is to by "faith and patience inherit the promises." We know, this is easier said than done because we are an impatient people. But wait in faith we must.

Once we begin to believe and "own" the word of the Lord to us, we must realize that God is working behind the scenes to bring the promised word to pass. Today, as in Scripture times, God works to change situations, change or replace people, move you or others to a new location, change relationships, and change entire groups of people to accomplish His word. We must realize that it takes the passage of time (a gestation period or season) to get everything and everyone in the proper place.

God's promises and prophetic and rhema words are *conditional* upon our response of faith. That word must be stood for, believed, contended for (I Tim. 1:18) and prayed into – from conception to completion. So stay in faith and patience, and God will get everything and everyone in the proper place in His time!

Be reminded: When God gives you a word – a rhema, a prophetic word, a prophetic dream, or a vision – it means He trusts you to receive and faithfully carry that promise or word to full activation. If the Holy Spirit did not trust you to receive and carry the word or promise, then He would not give it to you. So spend time with the Lord and be receptive to the word He wants to plant in your heart today and carry it with faith and patience!

3. CONFESSING with the Mouth

Romans 10:10b further states that "*with the **mouth** he confesses, resulting in salvation.*" For faith to work from the heart, the mouth must cooperate by speaking and agreeing. Speaking is a "possessor" of the truth.

Believing it in the heart, but not speaking it out of your mouth, is non-productive. James 2:26 says, "Faith without works is dead" – meaning it's inactive, not workable, non-productive, not useful, and worthless. Said another way, "faith without corresponding works is not fully activated." Words from the mouth reveal the *amount* of faith in the heart. Words are faith's measuring stick.

Living, biblical faith cannot fulfill its full function without your mouth speaking it. God's Word regarding your born-again spirit is voice-activated, so call it forth!

When a Christian says "I believe" in a certain biblical truth, and yet does not practice the scriptural principle, it is not faith, but simply acknowledging that the truth is valid.

> *I believed, therefore I spoke.* (2 Corinthians 4:13)

Declarations and Decrees

When you receive a word from the Lord, it must be contended for with your declarations and decrees to set things in motion in the spiritual realm. So contending becomes *your* assignment. When you contend by speaking, you give voice to the word, the will, and the ways of God.

> *In accordance with the prophecies previously made concerning you, that by them* [the prophetic words] *you fight* [contend] *the good fight* [warfare]. (I Timothy 1:18, brackets added)

A **declaration** is speaking a *truth* or a *promise* of Scripture. For example, if I say, "I am the righteousness of God in Christ Jesus," I am declaring *truth* about myself. If I say, "I can do all things through Christ who strengthens me," I am declaring a *promise* from Scripture that I am believing God to provide.

When you speak a **decree**, you are boldly speaking the *purposes* of God – something you believe God wants to accomplish that lines up with His will. For example, I can decree, "I will fulfill my God-given destiny." Or, "I decree that America will be saved and fulfill her God-given purpose."

Wake up the Word

There is an interesting story in Mark's gospel about Jesus and the disciples in a boat crossing the Sea of Galilee. Jesus fell asleep in the boat and a fierce storm came on them and the waves were filling the boat with water.

> *Jesus Himself was in the stern, asleep on the cushion; and they woke him and said to Him, "Teacher, do You not care that we are perishing?" And He got up and rebuked*

the wind and said to the sea, "Hush, be still." And the wind died down and it became perfectly calm. Mark 4:38-39

John 1:1-2 tells us that Jesus is the Word. When the disciples in the sinking boat woke up Jesus, they *woke up **the** Word*. You, too, are to "wake up the Word." You wake up the Word when you believe and speak the Word to bring the spiritual (in your born-again spirit) over into the physical and "make it your own."

The *"You Saids."* One highly effective way to wake up the Word is to talk about yourself — the 'real' you — the way God sees you and talks about you in His spiritual mirror. "Father, *You said* that I am the righteousness of God in Christ Jesus." "*You said* that I am completely forgiven of all my sins." Make it an on-going practice to believe, speak, and activate all that God has appropriated to you.

4. TAKING ACTION

If you really *believe* something in your heart and are *confessing* it with your mouth, then you must *take actions* that are in alignment with what you are saying you believe. Faith without corresponding action is useless (James 2:20).

You can determine how much faith you have by how much positive action you are taking in agreement with what is true about your born-again spirit.

How do you know or how can you tell when a truth is fully activated and complete in you?

- Your soul — mind, will, and emotions – are in 100% agreement and alignment with what has transpired in your born-again spirit
- You think, feel and talk about yourself in an upgraded way, and your habits display that upgraded view
- You can picture God's Word being true and settled in your mind's eye and you find inner rest in it; it's a done deal
- Others see it in your attitudes and actions.
- When a truth is fully activated in your soul, you are upgraded in that truth. It's a settled issue in your heart and mind, as that truth is now attached to your soul. You now have on-going victory in that area.

You are not double-minded about that truth in your heart. Double-minded means trust controls one part of your mind, and negativity (worry or doubt) controls the other, which is sometimes called a "fractured mind." Being single-minded means that you have an unfractured mind that is settled and whole, and at rest.

You are one step closer toward developing a righteousness conscious. Activation is repentance (repentance is changing the way you think) in action as you receive revelation and put off the old self and put on the new self. You are one step closer to being conformed to the image of Christ.

> Activation shows up in how you *think*, *feel* and *talk* about yourself, and in you *habits*.

Let's Ponder!

Have you stirred up [activated] the truths in your born-again spirit? Or, have you been neglecting to activate those truths?

What steps will you take so old things – mistakes, labels, lies — pass away from your born-again spirit, and are replaced with your full identity in Christ? Commit yourself to activate that spiritual reality in your understanding of yourself.

What are the "you saids" which you are going to believe and speak over your life during the next week? The week after that?

How do you know that a truth about your born-again spirit has been fully-activated in your soul?

Intersecting with Its Moment

As we shared previously, each word from the Lord has an assignment to complete. Each prophetic word or rhema word intersects with its moment so the assignment becomes active. This means words that the Lord quickens and makes alive to you need to intersect with their moment to become completely activated and operational. Prophetic words (infused and impregnated with a God assignment) must interact with their moment.

Right now, God is giving you words – rhema words, or prophetic words, or prophetic dreams, or visions – to believe so that Holy Spirit and His angels can activate them. So keep believing, speaking, and contending for each of those words to come to pass.

Let's decree together:

I decree all prophetic and rhema words are coming to their moment of activation.

I decree dreams and visions are connecting to their moment.

Here's the thing: you are already familiar with the Activation process. It's likely you have been practicing the Activation process in the wrong direction. You have been looking in the wrong mirror – *the I Am imposter* mirror — and believing and saying about yourself what your heavenly Father has *not* said is true about you. You may have been activating your mistakes, labels from others, lies from the enemy, and negative self-talk.

Reject those wrong images of yourself and choose to do the Activation process in the right direction. By faith, begin to *activate* what God has already placed in your born-again spirit by grace through the finished work of Christ. Choose to activate and positively respond to what God has already provided by grace.

Let's Internalize and Apply!

1. What does the term Activation mean?

_____

_____

_____

2. What are the four steps of Activation?

_____

_____

_____

3. Words have assignments on them. What does this mean?

_____

_____

_____

4. Where does faith function?

_____

_____

_____

5. What is a declaration? A decree?

6. How do you know or how can you tell when a truth is fully activated and complete in you?

7. What is meant by a word "intersecting with its moment?"

8. What is meant by the "You Saids"?

Chapter 8

It's a Balancing Act!

For by grace you have been saved through faith. . . (Ephesian 2:8a)

Grace and Faith: Activating What God Has Provided

Life is a balancing act. The Christian life is a proper balance of God's grace and our faith. Have you ever wondered what is God's part and what is your part in this relationship?

We have come to learn that *grace* is *God's* part based entirely on the finished work of Christ, and *faith* is *my* part in relationship with Him. Grace and faith work together to bring into manifestation what God has already provided in your born-again spirit. Being clear on this interaction is foundational to understanding the process of Activation. Let's take a quick look at both sides of this balancing act.

What Grace Is

Grace is the unearned, undeserved, and unmerited favor of God toward you. It is 100% what Jesus provided through His death, burial, resurrection, and seating at the right hand of the Father, and 0% of what you provided. It's *His* doing, not *your* doing.

> *For by grace you have been saved through faith; and that not of yourselves, it is the gift of God; not as a result of works, so that no one may boast. (Ephesians 2:8-9)*

Grace is something God did *for* you, apart from *you*.

By grace, Jesus died for the sins of the whole world. Prior to and independent of you or anything you could do to earn or deserve it, God provided your salvation and all that you will ever need.

For the grace of God has appeared, bringing salvation to all men. Titus 2:11

When you accept Christ as Savior, all that God provided for you was placed in your born-again spirit. Ask Holy Spirit to help you to discern what was placed in you as His empowering presence.

Faith and Believing

What Faith is Not

Faith is not something you do that makes God move. God doesn't respond to what we do "in faith" and then move. Faith does not make God do anything.

Religion says: "Faith is God responding to something that I do."

Truth: My faith doesn't move God; He is not stuck and needs a push. He is not the one who needs to move. Why? Because He moved nearly 2,000 years ago when He sent His Son to die on the Cross and give us the fullness of salvation.

God, through Christ, has provided what you will need and placed it into your born-again spirit.

So faith is not something you do to make God do something. The Bible calls this notion of "faith" *works* and *legalism*.

Let's Ponder!

Why does faith not move God?

What Faith Is

Faith is simply your positive response to what God has already provided by grace.

If what you are calling "faith" is *not* responding to what God has already done, then it's not true faith. Faith does not try to get God to positively respond to you. *True faith is your positive response to what God has already done by grace.*

Faith activates what God has already provided by grace.

If you are trying to make God do something new, then it's not true faith. The Christian life isn't waiting for God to do something new; He is waiting for you to respond positively to what He has already done! True faith only receives – reaches out and takes – what God has already done, already provided. It's receiving the benefits of the finished work of Christ and the fullness of the Holy Spirit.

> God is waiting for you to respond positively to what He has already done!

God has placed what you will need in your born-again spirit. For it to manifest, you simply must receive it through faith and *activate* the spiritual process of stirring up the gift which is within you. You don't have to make God give it; you just have to receive in the physical realm what He's already given you in the spiritual realm. Activate what God has already provided by grace.

Many people are asking God to do for them what He has already done. They're pleading with Him to give them what He's already given. Then, after praying this way in unbelief, they wonder why they aren't seeing the answer manifest.

Grace and faith work together to *activate* what God has already provided. You must believe that God has already done it. Then – by faith – reach over into the spirit realm and take *and activate* what's rightfully yours!

> Grace and faith work together to *activate* what God has already provided.

Sometimes it is hard to understand that everything God has already provided for you is in the spirit realm. Why? Because the physical realm does not exactly reflect what's true in the spirit realm. Faith acts as a *bridge* to bring what is true and real in the spiritual world into the physical world. We must provide that bridge. Reach over into the spiritual realm and bring what's already done into physical manifestation.

You may, at times, misunderstand the relationship between grace (God's part) and faith (your part).

Question: *Is God satisfied with you? Does He accept you?*

Answer: This is the wrong question. The real question should be: Is the Father satisfied with the cross of Jesus? Ephesians 1:6 NKJV says you are "accepted in the Beloved", and Romans 15:7 states "accept one another, just as Christ also accepted us to the glory of God." To the *extent* that God the Father is *satisfied* with and accepts Jesus' finished work, He is *satisfied with me*! In my born-again spirit, it is 100% His doing, and 0% my doing.

My Doing	His Doing
0%	100%

The original question (*Is God satisfied with you?*) puts the attention on *My Doing* when the real issue is on *His Doing* based on His finished work. Our adversary deceptively keeps trying to move our attention to the *My Doing* column rather than the *His Doing* column, putting the attention on self rather than Jesus.

We must keep the focus on the right side of the chart, *His Doing*. Now, in your born-again spirit, the Father is 100% satisfied with you based on the finished work of Christ.

A few more examples:

Question: *Is God pleased with you?*

To the extent that God the Father is <u>*fully pleased*</u> with Jesus' finished work, He is *fully pleased with you*!

Question: *Are you holy?*

To the extent that *Jesus is holy* in the eyes of His Father, you are holy in the eyes of your heavenly Father in your born-again spirit.

Question: *Are you righteous?*

To the *extent that Jesus is righteous* in the eyes of His Father, you are righteous in the eyes of your Heavenly Father. We hope you are understanding the sentence stem to answer these questions.

To summarize, faith is simply your positive response to what God has already provided by grace. Faith only activates what God has already provided in your born-again spirit by grace.

Let's Ponder!

If the Christian life is not waiting for God to do something, but waiting for you to respond positively to what He has provided, how can you reach out and receive what God has already provided?

As Jesus is NOW, so also are You in this World!

> . . .*as He is* [now], *so also are we* [in our born-again spirit] *in this world.* (I John 4:17, brackets added)

As Jesus Christ is *now*, so are you in your born-again spirit. Let that sink in. Your born-again spirit is—right now—as *perfect*, *mature*, and *complete* as Jesus Himself. Your born-again spirit is as perfect and complete as it'll ever be throughout all eternity. When God looks at you, He sees your born-again spirit that is as *righteous* and *holy* as Jesus.

To begin to see what has transpired in your born-again spirit, let's take a look at some of the truths about you.

Activating Your True Identity

As Jesus Christ is Now...	**So Am I in my Born-Again Spirit**
To the extent that Jesus is *righteous*...	I am *righteous* (Eph. 4:24; II Cor. 5:21)
To the extent that Jesus is *holy*...	I am *holy* (Eph. 4:24; I Cor. 3:17)
To the extent that Jesus is *totally accepted* by His Father...	I am *totally accepted* (Rom. 15:7) by my heavenly Father
To the extent that Jesus is *well pleasing* to His Father...	I am *well pleasing* my Father (Matt. 3:17; Mark 1:11)
As Jesus now is *perfect, complete, and mature*...	I am *perfect, complete, and mature* (Heb. 10:14; 12:23)
As Jesus is *crowned with honor and glory*...	I am *crowned with honor and glory* (Heb. 2:7)
To the extent that Jesus was *approved* by His Father...	I am *approved* (I Thess. 2:4)
As Jesus was *chosen* by His Father...	I am *chosen* (Col. 3:12; I Peter 2:9)

Remember, we are looking at how God our heavenly Father is looking at you. When the Father looks at you in your born-again spirit, He sees Jesus! The more you learn about who you are in your born-again spirit, the more you will discover about Jesus. Conversely, the more you learn about Jesus, the more you will discover about who you are in your spirit.

Let's Ponder!

Using the sentence stems from above, what are three statements you can tell yourself when you need to flip the script in your mind and remind yourself of who God says you are?

Let's Internalize and Apply!

1. What does the Bible mean by God's grace?

   _____

   _____

   _____

2. When I receive God's grace, what has God provided? Where is that provision located?

   _____

   _____

   _____

3. T/F: God's grace is only available to those who accept Jesus Christ as Savior. _____

4. What is it that faith in God does not do?

   _____

   _____

   _____

5. T/F: Faith is God responding to something that you do. _____

6. Faith that focuses on my works and actions is called _____?

7. Faith is your positive response to _____?

8. Faith only _____ what God has already provided by grace.

9. T/F: The Christian life is about waiting for God to do something new. _____

10. T/F: Praying in faith means pleading with God to give or provide an answer to your prayer. _____

11. What does it mean to activate what God has provided?

_____

_____

_____

Section 4:

Your True Identity

Let's now look deeper into the spiritual mirror of the Word of God to see what our Father sees when He looks at us. The members of the Godhead and all of heaven only see your new man in Christ. We will now learn what they see.

Your born-again spirit is a golden "treasure in an earthen vessel."

> *But we have this treasure in earthen vessels. . .* 2 Corinthians 4:7a

Jesus is the Treasure who lives in you as the new man. You are a new kind or race of man which in the likeness of God has been created righteous and holy (Eph. 4:24). You are now a member of a new race of people – the *saints* race.

You are a newly created person who did not exist before – a new kind of mankind that is – right now – as perfect, mature, and complete as Jesus Himself. As a member of the saints race, you are as perfect and complete as you will ever be throughout all eternity. Everything you'll ever need in your Christian life is already present in abundance in your born-again spirit. You are locked and loaded.

The war concerning our sins is over as far as heaven is concerned. This is such good news! The completeness of forgiveness is a truth that will transform you if you will receive the revelation of that forgiveness. You will view the Father in a different light — as loving, gracious, and good.

Repentance through the lens of the New Covenant is different than that of the Old Covenant. Falling short of the glory of God is different in the two covenants. You will discover the New Covenant view of repentance which is a freeing way to live!

Finally, the way that we think, feel, and talk about ourselves is very important. Too often we trip ourselves up with our words. We get hung by our tongue. We will learn the importance of speaking about ourselves the way all of heaven talks about us.

Chapter 9

What's True about Your Born-Again Spirit

Your spirit was instantly and completely transformed when you were born-again. Here are several key truths about your born-again spirit.

Truth #1: Everything that Christ has done for you at the Cross has already been deposited into your born-again spirit in fullness. You've already "Got it!"

Everything that God has done for you has already been deposited into your born-again spirit in abundance. It's there, so draw it out of your spirit and into the physical realm. You simply need the Spirit's revelation of what you already have!

> *For of His fullness we have all received, and grace upon grace.* John 1:16

> *For it was the Father's good pleasure for all the fullness to dwell in Him. . . For in Him all the fullness of Deity* [Father, Son, Holy Spirit] *dwells in bodily form, and in Him you have been made complete. . .* (Colossians 1:19; 2:9-10, brackets added)

> *seeing that His divine power has granted to us* <u>everything</u> *pertaining to life and godliness, through the true knowledge of Him who called us by His own glory and excellence.* (2 Peter 1:3, underline added)

You must see who you are and what you have in the spirit realm through the Word of God and believe it by faith. The Christian life is a process of renewing your mind and learning to release what you've already received in your born-again being.

The fruit of the Spirit is imparted into your spirit in *seed* form when you are *born* of the Spirit. The fruit are planted in your spirit as nine different *seeds* that are to be watered and cultivated until they grow to maturity in your heart. They are to infiltrate your nature and personality until they become your new nature and way of life. You've already "got it" and simply must activate and release each fruit of the Spirit.

Your Christian life is about learning how to manifest in the physical realm what's

already in your born-again spirit. You have the fullness of Christ, but the Lord also *imparts* additional gifts and graces of the Holy Spirit into you for effective ministry and Christian living. These additional gifts and graces of the Spirit empower you to fulfill your God-given destiny (Psalm 139:16). You have His fullness in your born-again spirit, so have an *abundance* mentality, and not a *deficit* (lack or deficient) mentality!

Let's Ponder!

How difficult is it for you to accept that everything you need has already been imparted into your spirit in abundance?

What does "you've already got it" include?

Truth #2: At this very moment, your born-again spirit is as perfect and complete as it'll ever be throughout all eternity.

You are *perfect* and *complete* in your born-again spirit! Your born-again spirit is sealed to keep out the impurities and evil, and seal in the new nature (which is righteous, holy, perfect, complete). When you were born-again, your spirit was encased – vacuum packed – by the Holy Spirit for preservation. Your born-again spirit retains its original holiness and purity – and will for eternity!

> *For by one offering He has <u>perfected</u> for all time those who are sanctified. . .and to the <u>spirits</u> of the righteous made <u>perfect</u>. (Hebrews 10:14; 12:23, underline added)*

As a Christian, when you sin, that sin cannot enter into your spirit but it can have a negative impact on your soul and body. Sin, if left unconfessed, can have an oppressive effect on your soul and ultimately on your body. It will also weigh heavily upon your spirit and fellowship with God and with other people.

You will not get a new born-again spirit when you arrive in heaven, and neither will it need to be matured, completed, or cleansed. Your born-again spirit down here is as perfect and complete as it'll ever be throughout all eternity.

Truth #3: Your born-again spirit is—right now—as *perfect, mature,* and *complete* as Jesus Himself.

You are a born-again spirit, you have a soul, and you live in a body. Your born-again spirit is the 'real' you which is as perfect, mature and complete as Jesus Christ. This should not be surprising because you received the spirit of Christ, God's holy Son, into your spirit when you were born again.

As long as we live on the earth, the temptation to sin will be a challenge. But when the Lord returns and takes us to heaven, then we shall be like Him not only in spirit, but in our soul and body as well.

Truth #4: When God looks at you, He sees your born-again spirit that is as *righteous* and *holy* as Jesus.

> *. . lay aside the old self* [the 'I AM imposter'], *. . .be renewed in the spirit of your mind, and put on the new self* [the 'I AM factor'], *which in the likeness of God has been created in <u>righteous</u> and <u>holiness</u> of the truth."* (Ephesians 4:22-24, underline and brackets added)

> *He made Him who knew no sin to be sin on our behalf, so that we might become the righteousness of God in Him.* (2 Corinthians. 5:21)

Let's unpack Ephesians 4:24 a little more: *. . .and put on the new* [not existing before] *self* [anthropos = new kind or race of man] *which in the likeness of God has been created* [made out of nothing physical] *in righteousness and holiness.*

You are now a member of a new race of people – the *saints* race, or the church race. You are part of a newly created people who did not exist before – a new superior kind of mankind now seated at the right hand of the Father. As a member of the saints race of people, you are superior to the first man, Adam. While Adam was created in innocence, you have been created in *righteousness*! And while Adam had authority and dominion over the earth, you have authority in *both* heaven and earth.

Your mortal body is here on earth, but your born-again spirit is seated with Christ Jesus at the right hand of the Father. It is a *mystery* and a *paradox* that you can be functioning in your natural body here on earth while at the same time your spirit is seated and functioning from the right hand of God in heavenly places in Christ!

Unfortunately, you (should I say *we*) will attempt to bring the old data (wrong self-image, culture, values) from our "old self" over and impose it upon the "new self" and it simply does not work. You must completely put off the old self and reprogram your soul with the "new self" of your born-again spirit.

God's spiritual mirror, His Word, perfectly reflects your born-again spirit, the 'real' you, which is how God the Father sees you!

Truth #5: When you sin, it does not originate from your born-again spirit. Your born-again spirit does <u>not</u> participate when you sin.

Your born-again spirit is *not* capable of committing sin. When your *spirit* and *soul agree*, you release and experience the *life* of God. The Christian life, by design, is intended to be a life of complete *dependence* on the Lord. This is where God wants us to live and walk.

> *Whoever has been born of God does not sin, for His* [Christ's] *seed remains in him; and he cannot sin, because he has been born of God.* (I John 3:9, NKJV, bracket added)

> *We know that no one who is born of God sins; but He* [Christ] *who was born of God keeps him, and the evil one does not touch him.* (I John 5:18, bracket added)

> "*. . .as He* [Christ] *is* [now], *so also are we in this world.*" (I John 4:17)

> *. . .for God cannot be tempted by evil, and He Himself* [in your born-again spirit] *does not tempt anyone.* (James 1:13, brackets mine)

However, when you choose to live *independent* of the Lord, your *body* and *soul agree* (apart from your born-again spirit) which closes the valve of the supernatural flow of life from your spirit; The result is sin. When you give in to temptation and sin, it originates from your flesh (soul + body), and not from your born-again spirit. You are defaulting to your old nature which is still present and dormant. When you give in to sin, your old nature is no longer dormant, because you are resurrecting it from the grave.

As a Christian walking in the flesh (a carnal Christian), you begin to walk like a lost person with your understanding darkened, and you separate yourself from the flow of the life of God within you.

When you sin, confess it right away! If you continue to sin, the love of God is not motivating your heart. Continuing to live in sin gives inroads for the devil to work in your life, violates unity and oneness with the Lord, and enslaves you once again. Thankfully, the Holy Spirit guides you to repent and not to repeat that sin in the future!

When you fail or sin (and we all occasionally do), you may think that God the Father is looking at your sin, but He is really looking at your born-again spirit, the 'real' you that is created in righteousness and holiness. Remember, the Father only sees one version of you, the new man (*anthropos*).

Again, your born-again spirit is *not* capable of sinning nor does sin originate from your spirit. As Jesus is NOW, so am I in this world – righteous, holy, perfect, and complete! This is not an excuse to sin, but should motivate you to stay pure in your Christian life!

Let's Ponder!

We learned that our born-again spirit is not capable of committing sin. How will you change your thinking so you see yourself as God the Father sees the 'real' you?

Your born-again spirit is as righteous, holy, perfect, and compete as Jesus. How difficult is it for you to believe that statement?

Truth #6, the very moment you were born again, you became as forgiven as you will ever be.

When you go to be with the Lord in heaven, you aren't going to get more cleansed. In your born-again spirit, you are as *perfect* and *holy* as you will ever be. You do have a body and soul that get defiled by sin in this life. Your conscience sometimes reverts back to the beliefs of your *I AM imposter*. However, your spirit is as born again as it will ever be. You are as clean, holy, and pure as Jesus himself in your born-again spirit. You continue to apply that forgiveness and live in freedom when you repent of anything that defiles your body and your soul.

> . . . *as He* [Jesus] *is* [now], *so also are we in this world.* (I John 4:17, brackets mine)

Let's Ponder!

As Jesus is now, so also are you in your born-again spirit. What will you do to internalize and embrace this truth?

How Do You See Yourself?

Respond to this statement:

>   True or False: "I am a sinner saved by grace."

How you answer this statement tells a great deal about how you see yourself.

If you answer TRUE. . .

> then as a Christian, you still see yourself as a *sinner*, having a *sin-consciousness* understanding of who you are. You still have an *inaccurate* understanding of your *I AM-ness*.

As a reminder, God only sees one version of you, the new man. He only has a righteousness view of you and doesn't see you as a sinner, but as a saint. He sees you as a learner, and not a loser or a failure. You need to see yourself the same way.

If you answer FALSE. . .

> then you are seeing yourself with a *righteousness-consciousness,* and you are beginning to have an accurate understanding of your *I AM-ness.*

We might correct the statement this way (the way God sees you now!):

> "I ~~am~~ *was* a sinner saved by grace; *now, I am a saint."*

You now stand on *righteousness-ground*, and no longer on condemnation-ground!

God sees the 'real you' (your born-again spirit) as *righteous, holy, perfect,* and *complete* as Jesus; therefore, you should as well.

The goal is to develop a righteousness consciousness where you no longer see yourself as a sinner (with a sin consciousness). Rather, you rightly see yourself as a righteous saint. (The term "saint" is a very frequent term for Christians in the New Testament.) You honestly and genuinely can say:

> "I no longer see myself as a sinner, but as a saint. . . who occasionally sins."

God does not see you as a 'sin' consciousness person; He sees you as having a 'righteousness' consciousness, since that is how He has recreated you! That's the gold standard.

Let's Internalize and Apply!

1. As a Christian, you are a born-again spirit, you have a soul, and you live in a body. So what is the 'real you'?

   _____
   _____
   _____

2. When God the Father looks at me, what does He see?

   _____
   _____
   _____

3. What is the difference between having a sin-consciousness and a righteousness consciousness? How can you move to having a righteousness consciousness, the gold standard?

   _____
   _____
   _____

4. What does it mean to "wear the name you've been given?"

   _____
   _____
   _____

5. When you sin (and we all do occasionally), does your born-again spirit participate?

_____

_____

_____

Chapter 10

The Completeness of Forgiveness

Jesus Christ. . . is the propitiation for our sins; and not for ours only, but also for those of the whole world. (I John 2:1-2)

One of the most important snapshots of your born-again spirit that you need to understand is:

"I am completely forgiven of all my sins – past, present, and future."

Lon speaking: *From my experience in ministry, this truth is one of the most difficult for many Christians to understand and accept as true. You, too, may find it hard to believe and accept that the "war" between you and God regarding your sins is over and God is not mad at you. I have found that once believers understand, believe, and accept this pivotal truth of complete forgiveness, the other truths are much easier to believe and activate. Therefore, this chapter is devoted to the subject of your complete forgiveness.*

So let's look into God's spiritual mirror of complete forgiveness. This chapter is a somewhat heavy chapter to read, but it is essential that you understand complete forgiveness in order to move forward.

First, God has forever settled the sin issue. God is not crediting (applying) sin against anyone. God has not credited sin to anyone for nearly 2,000 years. The sins of the entire world have been paid for but you only benefit from this if you repent when you do sin.

The rest of I John 2:1-2 states:

> *. . . and if anyone sins, we have an Advocate with the Father, Jesus Christ the righteous; and He Himself is the propitiation for our sins; and not for ours only, but also for those of the whole world.*

Not only are your sins as a Christian forgiven and paid for, the sins of the lost have been paid for as well. Jesus bore the sins of everyone – not just those He knew would accept Him. People aren't really going to hell because of sin. They're going to hell because they have rejected Jesus' payment for their sins.

If you think God is angry with you and is holding your sins against you, then you'll never have boldness, confidence, or faith. The truth of the matter is God is not angry with you about anything because you have been born again.

Jesus—who knew no sin, did no sin, and in Him was no sin — bore the condemnation of every sin ever committed. When Jesus ascended from the grave to sit at the right hand of the Father, there was no sin upon Him because He paid for all sin at the Cross. There is no sin upon us, either, because we are in Him. Your sins were left in the grave, because they did not make it through the resurrection.

You don't want to sin. But when you do, you are not condemned (I John 2:1 above) since your sins have already been judged and condemned at the Cross. When we sin, the Holy Spirit will convict us (not condemn us) to draw us back into unity with the Lord. Let us not grieve the Holy Spirit by failing to repent of a sin.

God does not hold a sin against you that Jesus has already paid for. If He did, God would be putting us in double jeopardy for a sin that Jesus already paid for.

> **God does not hold a sin against you that Jesus has already paid for.**

Second, you are forgiven of all sin – past, present, and future. God has forgiven you of all your sin, even sins you have not committed yet. God is no longer angry because you sin! Your forgiveness has been provided for and you *apply* that forgiveness when you confess a sin or failure.

> *. . .but through His own blood, He entered the holy place once for all, having obtained <u>eternal</u> redemption. . . those who have been called may receive the promise of the <u>eternal</u> inheritance.* (Hebrews 9:12c, 15, underline mine)

> *. . .we have been sanctified* [positionally] *through the offering of the body of Jesus Christ once for all. . . For by one offering He has perfected for all time those who are sanctified* [process]. (Hebrews 10:10, 14, brackets mine)

> *. . . and to the spirits of the righteous made perfect.* (Hebrews 12:23)

These verses show that you are forgiven of all past, present, and future sins *as you appropriate this truth.*

The Two-fold Work of Christ

As you can see in the illustration below, *The Salvation Triangle*[5], God has justified you based on the two-fold work of Christ. First, Christ rescued you from sin by *redeeming* you. Jesus redeemed you by purchasing you with His own blood. This is what *He did* in relation to you, not what you *do*.

Second, Christ turned aside the Father's wrath forever (called *propitiation*) regarding all of your sins through His sacrificial death. This is what Jesus did for us in relation to the Father. Jesus satisfied the righteous anger, wrath, and fiery indignation against all of your sins (Is. 53:10-11; 54:9-10). God the Father was fully satisfied with the payment of His Son on the cross and will never be angry with you. When it was completed, Jesus shouted, "It is finished!"

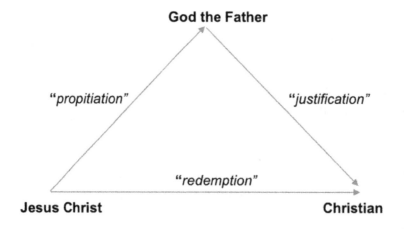

The Salvation Triangle]

---

[5] William Lasley, *Romans: Justification by Faith* (3rd Ed.), (Springfield, MO: Global University, 2010), 72

Jesus turned aside God's wrath, anger, and fury against sin through his sacrifice of atonement. Jesus permanently turned aside God's wrath through His sacrificial death. Jesus made a double payment – redemption and propitiation — for all sins for all time, taking the full brunt of the punishment you deserved, satisfying God's justice (Is. 40:2). Now, God is in total peace with you.

Lon speaking: *I've always understood that Jesus redeemed me as a result of His work on the Cross, but I did not understand His propitiatory work. When I committed a sin, I wrongly thought that if I did not quickly repent, God would be angry with me. As a result, I was not fully trusting the Father since I was sure that "the other shoe was going to drop" on me because of a sin for which I had not repented. I did not understand that Jesus took the full brunt of the Father's anger toward my sin and now if I do sin, it does not separate me from the Lord. Now, God is in total peace with me. The war is over!*

The good news is that on the basis of Christ's <u>redemptive</u> and <u>propitiatory</u> work, God is right in *justifying* you. All of your sins – past, present, and future–have been fully paid!

God's *holiness* is now on your side. His *righteousness* is now for you, not against you. You are His beloved in whom He is well pleased because of Jesus' finished work.

Let's Ponder!

What makes it difficult for you to see yourself as your Heavenly Father sees you – as righteous, holy, perfect and complete as you will ever be? Explain.

Do you find it hard to accept the truth that the sins you have committed are already forgiven?

When Jesus died on the cross for your sins, how many of them were in the future at that time?

Third, since you are born again, sin will never be an issue between you and God.

Question: Does this mean that you can just go live in sin?

Absolutely not! How shall you being dead in your relationship to sin return to revive the power of sin in your life? This would be returning to bondage. As a member of the saints race, you have been set free of the power of sin! You do not want to go back and live in sin.

Sin enslaves.

> *. . .when you present yourselves to someone as slaves for obedience, you are slaves of the one whom you obey, either of sin resulting in death, or of obedience resulting in righteousness?* Romans 6:16

> *Stand fast therefore in the liberty by which Christ has made us free, and do not be entangled again with a yoke of bondage.* Galatians 5:1 NKJV

Even though you are in Christ, the flesh remains dormant within you. In your born-again spirit, you are dead in your relationship to sin, so do not return to sin and revive it again! If you revive the flesh (your old nature), you resurrect it and it is no longer dormant. Choose to not walk according to the flesh (our old nature) but walk according to the Spirit (in our born-again spirit).

> *Even so consider yourselves to be dead to sin, but alive to God in Christ Jesus.* (Romans 6:11)

> **In your born-again spirit, you are dead in your relationship to sin, so do not return to sin and revive it again!**

Consider yourself dead to sin. The Father does.

You do not have to sin. To do so is to allow sin to "reign" in your mortal body. If you do, you certainly will not lose your salvation, but you will suffer the consequences of choosing to live *independent* of God. Do not get entangled again with a yoke (or attachment) to sin. If you sin, "crucify the flesh with its passions and desires" (Gal. 5:24). Put it to death! Your born-again spirit desires purity and liberty, that which is holy and righteous, so follow your spirit.

> *Having these promises, beloved, let us cleanse ourselves from all defilement of flesh and spirit, perfecting holiness in the fear of God.* (2 Corinthians 7:1)

Sinning violates the unity you have with the Lord and your spiritual oneness with Him.

You have the responsibility to safeguard your body from sin and keep it from being used as an instrument of unrighteousness. Failing to do so would be to *violate the unity* you have with the Lord and your spiritual oneness with Him. Sinning against your own body involves sinning against the one (Jesus) with whom you are united, allowing sin to reign in your mortal body.

> *. . .consider yourselves to be dead to sin, but alive to God in Christ Jesus. Therefore do not let sin reign in your mortal body so that you obey its lusts.* (Romans 6:11-12)

Has sin died? No, it is still present but dormant. In Christ, your relationship to sin has died. But when you give in to the temptation to sin as a Christian, you are once again giving sin power in your life by resurrecting it. The power of the flesh (soul + body) is strong and alluring, but when it makes its appeal, you don't have to respond. Choose to firmly resist temptation and preserve the unity you have with Jesus!

Sin gives an inroad for Satan to work in your life.

If you go out and live in sin, you're inviting Satan in. You're opening a door for the devil to work in your life.

Sinning is foolish. If you choose to live in sin, you're not smart. But God loves you. God is not holding your sin against you, but you are inviting the devil into your life. You are not going to prosper if you choose to live in sin. You will hinder, handicap, and even stop the blessing because you are not cooperating with God. You are called to freedom:

> *For you were called to freedom, brethren; only do not turn your freedom into an opportunity for the flesh, but through love serve one another.* (Galatians 5:13)

Fourth, God does not impute (hold) sin against you and will not hold future sin against you.

> *. . .just as David also speaks of the blessing on the man to whom God credits* [imputes] *righteousness apart from works: Blessed are those whose lawless deeds have been forgiven* [past tense], *and whose sins have been covered* [past tense]; *Blessed is the man*

Activating Your True Identity

whose sin the Lord will not [future tense] *take into account* [impute sin]." (Romans 4:6-8, brackets added)

This verse says God "will not" impute (credit) *sin* to you, because He has already imputed *righteousness* to you. When you were born again, all of your sins – past, present, and even future sins – were laid on Jesus. God will never in the future hold sins against you! When you do sin, it is your responsibility to confess that sin and thank God that this sin has already been forgiven. In so doing, you are not letting sin negatively affect your heart, your body, and your relationships.

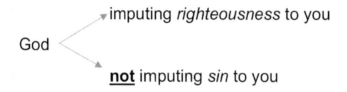

Christ's finished work is not benefiting you if you fall into religious thinking that says,

> "I've been saved by grace, but now that I am a Christian, I need to pray, fast, tithe, study, and attend church in order for God to love me, bless me, use me, and answer my prayers."

You know that God is powerful, but you may think, "How could He ever use His power on my behalf?" This puts you back under a sin-consciousness rather than a righteous-consciousness, thinking you have to perform to keep God's favor. You begin to doubt God's willingness to use His ability on your behalf because you feel He is still holding sin against you.

This is religion speaking and not the Bible. Religion puts the focus on what *you* need to do instead of what *Christ* has already done. Religion is all about your "doing" – that's behavior modification.

Your acceptance is found at the Cross because the Father was fully satisfied with Jesus' payment for your sins. Now, your heavenly Father assesses you based on what Jesus has already done. When you do sin, repent and thank Him that this sin is forgiven.

To the extent that God the Father is *satisfied* with Jesus' finished work, He is *satisfied with you!*

Question: *Is God satisfied with you?*

Answer: This is the wrong question. The real question should be: Is the Father satisfied with the cross of Jesus?

Ephesians 1:6 NKJV says you are "accepted in the Beloved", and Romans 15:7 states "accept one another, just as Christ also accepted us to the glory of God."

The original question (*Is God satisfied with you?*) puts the attention on *My Doing* when the real issue is on *His Doing* based on His finished work. Our adversary deceptively keeps trying to move our attention to the *My Doing* column rather than the *His Doing* column, putting the attention on self rather than Jesus (refer to illustration in chapter 8). We must keep the focus on the right side of the chart, *His Doing*. It's about *His* doing, and not *your* doing.

Being and Doing. Your adversary wants you to mix up your *being* with your *doing*. As a Christian, you first must *be* holy (I Pet. 1:16) in your born-again spirit, before you can *live* holy (I Pet. 1:15). Because all your sins are completely forgiven (based on *His Doing*), there is nothing you can add (My Doing) to cause God to love and fully accept you. Be watchful, for your adversary would like for you to think that it was, say, 90% *His Doing*, and 10% *My Doing*. No, it has always been *100% His Doing*.

In summary, God placed all your sin upon Jesus. All your sin. Sin is a non-issue with God. He is aware of it and will strongly impress upon you to quit doing it, but not because He's going to reject you. He's already paid for it. God is not ignorant of sin in your life (it's the point of a future upgrade!), but it does not change His attitude toward you. He paid for your sin – past, present, and even future sins. When God looks at you, He sees your born-again spirit – which is as eternally righteous and holy as Jesus!

What I may have done (sin, failure) is *not* who I am. My actions or wrong thinking do not define my identity in Christ. What God has said about me, and provided through Jesus Christ, defines my identity.

> My actions or wrong thinking do not define my identity in Christ. What God has said about me, and provided through Jesus Christ, defines my identity.

> ### Let's Ponder!
>
> *Do you feel that God is imputing or holding a sin against you? If so, are you thinking with a 'sin consciousness' or with a 'righteousness consciousness?'*
>
> *How can you flip the script to see God imputing righteousness to you?*

Fifth, God does not put a timeline on your forgiveness!

Every time you sin, the Lord doesn't have to wait until you repent in order to get that sin under the Blood and then be forgiven. Our redemption in Christ was not a short-term redemption – that is, only good until the next time you sin (and then have to repent, get the Blood reapplied, and be forgiven again).

The truth is Christ entered the holy place once and obtained for us an *eternal* redemption. God's grace is *cheapened* when you think He has only forgiven you of your sins up to the point you are saved, and after that point, you must depend on your confession of sins to be forgiven. God's forgiveness is not given in *installments*.

If you believe God's forgiveness is given in installments, you won't be able to expect God to protect, provide, and prosper you. It will rob you of your ability to receive God's goodness, blessings, unmerited favor, and success.

> **God's forgiveness is not given in installments.**

Lon speaking: *This truth about no timeline on forgiveness was very difficult for me to accept for a number of years. I felt that my sins were forgiven up to a point – up to the most recent time that I confessed my sins – but not since that time. I felt He was still holding these latter sins against me. This is what religion had taught me and not the Bible. Religion had put the focus on what I needed to do instead of what Christ has already done.*

I was living with a sin consciousness with a pretty strong emotional attachment to that wrong understanding. I was listening to the wrong voice (religion) rather than God's voice that says I am completely forgiven of all my sins – past, present, and future. Now, I have the Spirit's revelation of the completeness of God's forgiveness. I am free to live with a righteousness consciousness in my born-again spirit; I am <u>completely</u> forgiven!

So now when I sin, I quickly repent of it out of my love for the Lord and thank Him that this sin has been forgiven on the Cross two-thousand years ago. I rejoice that my loving heavenly Father forgave me of all my sins and I appropriate that forgiveness when I repent!

Let's Ponder!

Do you put a timeline on God's forgiveness of your sins?

Do you feel that God has only forgiven you up to a point in time?

Moving forward, how can you regularly appropriate God's forgiveness on an on-going basis?

Sixth, God has completely qualified us in our standing before Him! He has qualified us for all His blessings through the shed blood of Jesus Christ on the cross, and His burial and resurrection.

> *giving thanks to the Father, who has qualified us to share in the inheritance of the saints in Light.* (Colossians 1:12, underline added)

You are fully qualified to share in the full inheritance that is yours!

Don't fall into the trap of looking at your life, imperfections and failings, and start to disqualify yourself from receiving God's blessings and favor. You may be tempted to think, "Why would God bless me? Look at what I've done. I am so underserving."

Instead of having faith to believe God for breakthroughs, you may feel too condemned to be able to believe in God's goodness and to receive what He has already provided when He qualified you.

All your *disqualifications* exist in the *natural* realm. You live and operate in the *supernatural* (spiritual) realm where God has *qualified* you with His favor. God has fully qualified you in your born-again spirit.

Say out loud: "I am fully qualified to share in His inheritance!"

Let's summarize: Because of the finished work of Christ at Calvary, God has not credited, or imputed, sin against anyone for nearly 2,000 years. What God has imputed to you is "everlasting righteousness" (Dan. 9:24). Christ paid for all sins – past, present, and even future for every person for all time. The war is over. God is no longer angry because of your sin. Your sin is no longer an issue with God.

Let's Ponder!

What are some of the ways you disqualify yourself from God's blessings?

How can you flip the script and walk in the truth that you are fully qualified in the eyes of your heavenly Father?

Let's Internalize and Apply!

1. Are the sins I commit an issue for God the Father? Why or why not?

   _____

   _____

   _____

2. When you were born again, how many of your sins were forgiven? Today, how many of your sins are forgiven? Which of your sins today are unforgiven?

   _____

   _____

   _____

3. Does God put a timeline on His forgiveness of your sins?

   _____

   _____

   _____

4. If you die as a Christian with unconfessed sin, do you go to heaven or hell?

   _____

   _____

   _____

Chapter 11

The Gift of a Good Conscience

But the goal of our instruction is love from a pure heart and a good conscience and a sincere faith.
(1 Timothy 1:5)

One of the wonderful gifts that the Father has provided us through the finished work of Christ is the gift of a good conscience. In the verse above, the apostle Paul stated that a having a good conscience and pure heart before God is foundational to walking in love and faith. If you don't have an accurate and upgraded conscience before God, then you will have a distorted and incomplete view of your true identity in Christ. This will interfere with your relationship with God – not feeling fully accepted by Him. You have already learned that you are totally accepted by the Father; let that truth be fully activated in your heart!

The lack of a good conscience can also affect your relationships with others. The apostles Paul and Peter declare the lack of a good conscience before God can negatively affect your relationship with others (1 Tim. 1:19; 1 Pet. 3:16). Not feeling fully accepted by the Father can open the door of feelings of rejection by others.

How do you develop a good conscience before God?

You develop a good conscience by having a scriptural understanding of two things: the completeness of your forgiveness by the Father (the previous chapter) and the gift of no condemnation.

We will learn about this wonderful gift of no condemnation and followed by what is required to have a good conscience.

God the Father has given you the *gift of no condemnation!*

> *Therefore, there is now no condemnation for those who are in Christ Jesus. . . Who is the one who condemns?* Romans 8:1, 34

God has given you the *gift of no condemnation*! The more you start (1) to believe that you are righteous in Christ and (2) refuse to accept condemnation for your past mistakes and present temptations, the more you will be set free from hindrances and addictions that bind you.

Even though you fail, there is no condemnation because you are in Christ and all your sins were washed away by His Blood. When God looks at you, He doesn't focus on your failures. God sees you as a *learner*, not a failure. As Jesus is spotless and without blame, so are you in your born-again spirit (the 'real' you)! Remember, as Jesus is now, so are you in this world (I Jn 4:17).

> God sees you as a *learner*, not a failure.

Make this declaration out loud:

> I am *free from condemnation* because Jesus has given me the gift of no-condemnation!

If you feel condemned, it is not from God. Your own conscience may smite you, and Satan – the accuser of the brethren – may condemn you, but God does not.

When you do something wrong, you will sense a conviction from the Holy Spirit to repent of that sin. However, the feeling of condemnation is different – it's an *assault* against your sonship in Christ. That assault is either from Satan or your conscience, but it is not from God. Conviction from the Holy Spirit leads you to repentance and draws you into purity in your fellowship with the Lord; condemnation leads you to despair and hopelessness.

Condemnation does not come from the Godhead! God the Father, nor Jesus, nor the Holy Spirit are condemning you (Romans 8:31-35). Your own heart may condemn you, and you may have blamed it on God. But God is *not* angry with you. God is not out to "get you." He is not even in a bad mood. God loves you! The Lord is truly at peace with you!

Remember, God the Father has given you the *gift of no condemnation*, which gives you the power to overcome your weaknesses and failures!

Let's look now at how to reject condemnation and develop a good conscience.

Condemnation Source #1: Our Enemy

> *No weapon that is formed against you will prosper; And every tongue that accuses you in judgment you will condemn. This is the heritage of the servants of the Lord, And their vindication* [righteousness] *is from Me, declares the Lord.* (Isaiah 54:17, bracket added)

We often quote this verse, but we should start at the end of the verse: you are declared righteous! That is an identity statement. Knowing that you are righteous in your born-again spirit enables you to confidently condemn and firmly reject every tongue of accusation, judgment, and condemnation that rises against you.

Action Step: Start speaking and maintaining your belief and confession that you are righteous. Use your faith for the most important thing — believing that you are righteous in Jesus by faith.

The enemy pours accusation on you using the *voice of a legalist* to disqualify you. He uses the voice of religion to accuse. The enemy uses the law and commandments to show your failures, and to put a *spotlight on how your behavior has disqualified you* from fellowship with God, pointing out how undeserving you are of His acceptance, love, and blessings. He uses the law to heap condemnation upon you and give you a sense of guilt and distance from God. Your enemy knows that the more condemnation and guilt you experience, the more likely you are to feel alienated from God and continue in sin. (Remember, you are *fully qualified* to participate in His inheritance; embrace it!)

However, you should not allow the devil to condemn you for not keeping the Law; for the Law is for the unbeliever, and not for the righteous person.

> *But we know that the Law is good, if one uses it lawfully, realizing the fact that law is not made for a righteous person, but for those who are lawless and rebellious, for the ungodly and sinners, for the unholy and profane. . .* (I Timothy 1:8-9c)

If you will accept, believe, and rest in your identity in Christ, and live and walk in the Holy Spirit, you will supernaturally keep, and even exceed, the requirements of the Law. Focusing on the law keeps us aware of sin, but focusing on righteousness by grace leads to freedom from condemnation!

The Litmus Test

The voice of accusation and condemnation only works if your adversary can get you to focus on *your* doing rather than *His* doing.

My Doing		His Doing
Self-occupied	vs:	Christ occupied
Self-conscious	vs:	Christ conscious
Me	vs:	my identity in Christ
My doing	vs:	Christ's doing/finished work

God is no shamer or fault-finder. He is no longer angry!

Another Action Step: *Put the spotlight on the finished work of* Christ, who on the Cross took your condemnation and qualified you to receive God's acceptance, love, and favor forever!

Receive the gift of no condemnation, as it will give you the power to overcome your weaknesses and failures!

Condemnation Source #2: A conscience not fully transformed to a 'righteousness consciousness' belief system.

Since you are born-again, you will need to reprogram your conscience. Your conscience may have been programmed with a wrong belief system (from the old self or religion) based on dead works or an evil conscience, and needs to be upgraded.

> *...how much more will the blood of Christ . . . cleanse your <u>conscience</u> from <u>dead works</u> to serve the living God?* (Hebrews 9:14, underline added)

> *...let us draw near with a sincere heart in full assurance of faith, having our hearts sprinkled clean from an <u>evil</u> <u>conscience</u>...* (Hebrews 10:22, underline added)

Let's look at what these terms mean.

Dead works = the notion that God's acceptance is based on your performance (*My Doing*), rather than what Jesus has done with your sins.

Your spirit was cleansed of its sin nature, but you may not have purged your conscience with the truth about what Jesus has done with your sins. Satan is dragging up things you have done. Don't allow your own negative self-talk or the devil's condemnation to destroy your faith and confidence in God because you think you don't deserve His forgiveness and favor. *Reject* the lie that your acceptance by God is based on what you do and *embrace* that He accepts you based 100% on Jesus' finished work.

Evil conscience = the notion that your core self (your spirit) as a Christian is still sinful; you still have a *sin-consciousness* rather than a *righteousness-consciousness*.

You have the Gospel – the Good News! God has given you what you don't deserve (His grace) and He is not angry with you or holding your sin against you. Jesus paid for all of your sins – past, present, and even the ones you haven't committed yet. All of your sins have been forgiven. Make this declaration out loud:

"I am as *righteous* and *holy, perfect* and *complete* as Jesus.

You need to embrace a *righteousness-consciousness* view of who you are! This will give your conscience a much-needed upgrade!

Let's Ponder!

When you sin, do you ever feel condemned? How should you respond?

What does it mean to have a "righteousness-consciousness?"

Let's Internalize and Apply!

1. When you feel condemned, what is/are the source(s)?

   _____

   _____

   _____

2. What are dead works? How do you cleanse your conscience of "dead works?"

   _____

   _____

   _____

3. What is meant by an "evil conscience?" What is the remedy for an evil conscience?

   _____

   _____

   _____

4. Will your born-again spirit be further "cleansed" when you get to heaven?

   _____

   _____

   _____

Chapter 12

An Upgraded View of Repentance

With an upgraded view of the Father towards you and the finished work of Christ, let's see what repentance looks like.

Under the new covenant, manifesting the fruit of the Spirit is the way you demonstrate the glory of God. When you fail to manifest the fruit of the Spirit, the nature of Christ, you fall short of the glory of God.

So what does repentance look like under the New Covenant?

Repentance for the new man is entirely different in the secret place of being in Christ.

The Father is saying:

> *Because you are living in the new man, you have to learn to repent as the the new man because the old place of repentance has passed away. A place of new repentance is here.*
>
> *Under the old covenant, people repented for doing wrong. All that has passed away. Jesus fulfilled that law in Himself by being the sinless sacrifice!*
>
> *Instead, in the new covenant, you can only repent of failing to do what is right in the nature of Jesus! Sin in the new covenant is defined as falling short of My glory. When you **default** to a response of the old man that is less than who We are for you, you fall short of My glory. Repentance restores you to the place of increase and fullness.*

The fruit of the Spirit is a by-product of the relationship you have with the Holy Spirit. The fruit of the Spirit was imparted into your spirit in *seed* form when you were *born* of the Spirit. The fruit were planted in your life as nine different *seeds* that are to be watered and cultivated until they grow to maturity: *love, joy, peace, patience, kindness, goodness, faithfulness, gentleness, self-control* (Gal. 5:22–23).

The fruit of the Spirit needs to infiltrate your nature and personality until they become your new nature and way of life.

If you don't allow the fruit of the Spirit to have full expression, then you are living below the line or level of privilege in your life in the Spirit.

The new way of repentance works like this:

Let's say God is working to upgrade the **fruit of *peace*** in your soul but you keep defaulting to your previous habit of anxiety and impatience. Jesus took anxiety and impatience away on the Cross. It is *unhelpful* to repent of something God had already declared to be dead.

Instead, repentance sounds like this:

"Father, thank You for giving me a great opportunity to walk in the fruit of the Spirit of peace. I repent that I did not practice Your peace and came up short of Your glory, and missed the opportunity to be Christ-like. I ask You to give me another occasion soon to increase peace in my life."

Doesn't that sound so much better?

No guilt or shame that goes with the old man.

The Father is saying:

> *There is no need to condemn yourself. Instead, We are stirring in you a gentle, joyful willingness to realize the benefit of the next opportunity and then be ready for it! Repentance creates a delight in you for the process of transformation that We love to create in you.*

If you simply confess that you missed the opportunity to be Christ-like, to manifest the fruit of the Spirit, please know He is faithful and just to forgive you and cleanse you of not doing what is right.

Therefore, to one who knows the right thing to do and does not do it, to him it is sin [falling short of the glory of God by not manifesting the fruit of the Spirit]. (James 4:17, bracket added)

> *If we confess our sins* [of falling short of the glory of God], *He is faithful and righteous to forgive us our sins and to cleanse us from all unrighteousness* [for falling short of the glory of God]. (I John 1:9, brackets added)

And, no worries, you will be given another opportunity to become like Jesus because the secret place in Him is also the place of love and safety! Repentance is your privilege because, in the new man context, it is also a reminder of how the Father sees the real you in His beloved Son.

> **It is *unhelpful* to repent of something God had already declared to be dead.**

Again, it is not helpful for you to repent in line with something that God has declared to be dead. To repent towards your new nature in Jesus fixes your attention on what God is doing in you now to manifest His nature through the fruit of the Spirit. This moves you forward into your identity in Christ.

God loves repentance that renews your expectation of goodness. It is impossible to see God's glory through the eyes of the old man. But in the new man, His glory is always present.

Let's Ponder!

What if you are never challenged by circumstances, but by the fruit of the Spirit?

What if the fruit of the Spirit is more effective against the enemy than the gifts of the Spirit?

Let's Internalize and Apply!

1. What does falling short of the glory of God mean in the New Covenant?

   _____

   _____

   _____

2. When you repent, what are you to confess?

   _____

   _____

   _____

3. T/F: It is unhelpful to repent of something God has already declared to be dead. _____

Chapter 13

Don't Get Hung by Your Tongue

The Power of Words

God's Word regarding your born-again spirit is voice-activated. Words create everything (Hebrews 11:3). Words are the parent force. Everything responds to words. So, start speaking the favor God has spoken over you!

There is tremendous power in words. With the tongue you can either bless or curse, that is, speak life or death.

> *Death and life are in the power of the tongue.* (Proverbs 18:21)

> *I have set before you life and death, the blessing and the curse. So choose life in order that you may live, you and your descendants. . .* (Deuteronomy 30:19)

It is helpful to think that each spiritual truth about your born-again spirit contains a packet of *positive spirit* and *life*. Jesus said, "It is the Spirit who gives life; the flesh profits nothing; the words that I have spoken to you are spirit and are life (John 6:63).

Conversely, a curse – a negative label someone spoke over you, a mistake you made that you have named yourself, or a lie from the enemy – also contains a packet of a *negative spirit* and *death*. A negative emotional feeling will accompany this curse, manifesting as a sense of shame, unworthiness, guilt, or condemnation.

- Have you ever made a mistake, for example, offended someone with your words; or yelled at your friend, spouse or child in anger; or did something disrespectful; or walked out on a relationship? A mistake is an event; it is not your identity!

- Or perhaps you have believed the labels that others have spoken over you: you're just average, or inferior, not capable, have an addiction, or you're a loser.

- Maybe you have believed some of the lies the enemy has whispered in your ear, such as you don't have what it takes, you're not talented or special, or you don't measure up.

If you dwell on any of these too long, you begin to believe them and identify with them, and you think of them as your name. When this happens, you are looking in the wrong mirror and at the wrong image. A name is a powerful thing.

Whether you know it or not, people's words have had influence in your life.

Maybe you left home cursed and wearing a negative label. You were told,

> "You're a failure! You can't do anything right. You're never going to make it. You're not going to amount to anything."

It could have come from a parent, or perhaps a counselor, or a coach, or an ex from a prior relationship who cursed you and your future. There is power in words.

Negative words create a wrong image on the inside regarding who you are. Such negative labels distort the 'real' you and contribute to the I AM imposter mindset. You begin to see yourself as a *victim*, rather than a *victor* in Christ.

The good news is before someone put a curse (negative label) on you, God had already put His commanded blessing on you. Our heavenly Father has blessed us with every spiritual blessing in the heavenly places in Christ (Eph. 1:3). The blessing supersedes, overrides, and reverses the curse.

There is a story in the book of Numbers where a king contracted with a prophet named Balaam to speak a curse on the children of Israel as they were approaching the Promised Land. Balaam told the king that he would only speak what God told him to say. Balaam said: *"Behold, I have received a command to bless; when He has blessed, then I cannot revoke it." How shall I curse whom God has not cursed? And how can I denounce whom the Lord has not denounced?"* (Numb. 23:8, 20).

There is power in a blessing that God has spoken over you. And that blessing is much greater than a curse, but you have to believe it.

Unfortunately, you can believe a curse too. A curse doesn't have any effect unless you submit to it. Satan curses you. People curse you, trying to put a negative label on you. They say bad things about us all the time. But unless you respond to a curse in fear and believe it, it won't stick.

. . .so a curse without cause does not alight. (Proverbs 26:2)

A curse doesn't have any power over you unless you believe it, unless you fear it. Fear is nothing but faith in a negative, faith in the wrong thing. You have to empower that curse over you by believing it.

For words of other people to affect you and bring life or death, you have to believe them. Likewise, the favor of God – the blessing He has spoken over you – has to be believed in order for its power to be released. Do you believe in the power of a blessing?

When someone tries to curse you with a negative label, let it go in one ear and out the other. Don't believe it, accept it, or let it land on you.

Let's Ponder!

What are some ways words of others have impacted you positively?

Impacted you negatively?

You have the power to bless your own life and future. But sometimes, you curse your own life and future.

So many people are "hung by their tongue." They're just speaking what they feel, saying,

"Well, they say it's a downturn in the economy and everybody is getting laid off. I'm sure that if they lay off workers, I'll be one of the first."

By talking that way, you're cursing yourself – putting a negative label on yourself.

> "Well, I can't do anything right. I don't have what it takes. I don't have the education. I have the wrong background. We lived on the wrong side of the tracks."

These are all curses and you're the one empowering them.

If You Say So

The scripture tells us that there is something more dangerous than eating something bad: speaking out something that is bad (Matt. 15:11).

When God hears you speak about your meeting with coworkers as terrible, your car as crappy, your kids as ungrateful, your husband as lazy, your town as small, your house as cramped…His response is: *If you say so.* You will experience what you speak.

Likewise, there is power in speaking out something that is good.

At creation, God spoke the world to life. At the incarnation, God spoke Jesus into our world. That tells you something about the impact of words. And it should humble you to know that God has given you the same power of speech. That is part of the privilege of being made in His image. You have great power in your words that can unleash a forceful fury that can create, tear down, build, heal, or hurt.

An interesting story in Matthew 8 shows what we are trying to communicate. A centurion came to Jesus for help because his servant was seriously ill. In verse 13, Jesus said, "Go; it shall be done for you as you have believed." This was Jesus' way of saying the word *Amen,* meaning "let it be so." When you say amen you are saying, "may what I have prayed come to pass." Your goal should be to make bold declarations about who you are that, with raised eyebrows, God would say to you: Amen, let it be so.

It is up to you whether the self-fulfilling prophecies you speak become a delight or a burden. God's response to the way you speak is: "If you say so."

> ### *Let's Ponder!*
>
> *How do I speak to myself and others? In what way is my speech positive?*
>
> *In what ways do I have a hard time controlling my tongue?*
>
> *Think of an area of your life you tend to complain about or speak negatively of. Challenge yourself this week, every time you are tempted to complain, to find a way to thank God instead.*

***Unforgiveness* and *hatred* also empower the curse and stop the blessing.**

You are the one empowering the curse when you won't let go of the offense you took because of how someone else treated you. It closes the *valve* and stops the flow of God's blessing.

You need to start empowering the truth about your born-again spirit by faith and quit fearing the curse. Let's stop fearing what people have said about us and what they have done to us and start walking in the blessing of God!

> ### *Let's Ponder!*
>
> *By your words, are you putting a curse or a negative label on your life?*
>
> *Your future?*
>
> *Your family members?*
>
> *Do you see how putting a curse or a negative label on yourself undercuts the process of activating in your soul what is already in your born-again spirit?*

God wants you to break those curses over your life and stop them from working against you. But you have to denounce them and condemn them.

> *"No weapon that is formed against you will prosper; And every tongue that accuses you in judgment you will condemn. This is the heritage of the servants of the Lord, And their vindication is from Me," declares the Lord.* Isaiah 54:17

You have to say,

"No longer will this curse dominate me. I'm going to receive the blessing of God!"

Out loud, read this prayer and highlight the words that stand out for you.

Model prayer:

"Father, I repent of empowering these curses by believing what others have said about me. Forgive me for being hurt and offended when You've said so many wonderful things about me. You have blessed me. I am blessed above all people on the face of the earth (Deut. 7:14). I repent of letting these curses, these negative words, dominate me. Right now, I take authority in Christ Jesus, and I speak death to those curses. In the name of Jesus, I say that I am not going to let any curse that anyone has spoken over me – or that I have spoken over myself – to remain. I break them all, in Jesus' name. I can do all things through Christ who strengthens me (Phil. 4:13). You always cause me to triumph in the Lord Jesus Christ (2 Cor. 2:14). I am above only and not beneath. I am the head and not the tail (Deut. 28:13).

I break the curses of doctors, bankers, lawyers, and any other person who has spoken negative things – death words – to me about who I am as a person. I renounce those curses in the name of Jesus and refuse to allow them to dominate me anymore.

Father, I believe what you have said about me. Your blessing is stronger than any curse and, right now, I activate Your blessing by faith. From this time forth, I am blessed of the Lord (Psalm 115:15). It is the blessing of the Lord makes me rich, and You add no sorrow to it (Prov. 10:22). I am blessed coming in and blessed going out (Deut. 28:6). I'm blessed in my basket and in my storehouse (Deut. 28:5). Thank you that everything I set my hand to is blessed (Deut. 28:8).

I speak the blessing of God over my life, and I break the curse. From this moment forward, the curse in my life has ended, and it's the beginning of the blessing. I declare it by faith in Jesus' name. Amen!

> ## Let's Ponder!
>
> *How can you develop a favor-consciousness?*
>
> *How can you begin to bless your life? Your family? Your future?*

Meditation in the Bible involves giving "voice" to the Scripture you are dwelling on.

> *This book of the law shall not depart from your mouth, but you shall meditate* [hagah = to mutter] *on it day and night... for then you will make your way prosperous, and then you will have success.* (Joshua 1:8, brackets added)

> *But his delight is in the law of the Lord, And in His law he meditates* [hagah = to mutter] *day and night.* (Psalms 1:2, brackets added)

"*Hagah*" simply means "to mutter." It means to take God's Word and chew on it, to savor it, to ruminate on it, and speak it.

> *...my heart grew hot within me. While I meditated* [hagah], *the fire burned; then I spoke with my tongue.* (Psalm 39:3 NIV, brackets added)

Meditation does not mean vain repetition, but as you are dwelling on God's Word about who you are, ask the Holy Spirit to give you a fresh revelation of what has transpired in your born-again spirit. Let the Scripture burn with revelation in your heart. And as you speak out of the burning revelation, God anoints the words you speak. Now, you have *power* in your declaration about your identity in Christ!

To meditate essentially means to speak it to yourself. Speak it over and over. Reflect on every word and let each one feed and nourish you. In so doing, you will elevate yourself into the presence of the Lord!

You activate what you believe when you speak, out loud, every good thing in your born-again spirit in Christ. Speak every good thing that you *are*, you *have*, and *can do* in Christ!

Let's Ponder!

What truths can you begin to "mutter" to acknowledge every good thing which is in you in Christ Jesus?

What is true of your born-again spirit that you can "mutter" about who you <u>are</u>?

About what you <u>have</u>?

About what you <u>can do</u>?

Let's Internalize and Apply!

1. In our study, what is meant by our words being the "parent force"? How are God's blessings activated?

   _____

   _____

   _____

2. In order for words to have the effect of a curse, what has to happen?

   _____

   _____

   _____

3. What can hinder or stop the flow of God's blessings?

_____

_____

_____

4. What is meant by "meditation" in the Bible?

_____

_____

_____

SECTION 5:

Activating Your Identity At A Deeper Level

So far, you have discovered that the Activation process helps to upgrade your soul with the truth about your born-again spirit. As these truths are activated in your soul by transforming your mind, you will also need to keep your soul clean and pure in the sight of God and others.

In this section, we will focus on your soul. You will discover several processes and tools to assist in removing negativity from your soul, keeping it clean and unencumbered from these weights. You will learn the Recircuiting Process and the steps to do a Soul Check-up.

You will learn a biblical perspective of your circumstances, situations, and problems and how God wants to use them to upgrade your identity.

Finally, you will learn the major way that Holy Spirit can upgrade you for ministry through the uploading and downloading process.

Chapter 14

Recircuiting Your Mind

Let us lay aside [renounce] *every weight* [wrong perception],
and the sin which so easily ensnares us, and let us run with endurance the race that is set before us.
(Hebrews 12:1 NKJV, brackets added)

As you have learned, the Activation process is about your soul catching up to what has already transpired in your born-again spirit. Your soul consists of your mind, will, and emotions. For soul-health, it is imperative to think and speak with a renewed mind concerning your true identity and to live a victorious life in the Spirit.

Your conscious mind as well as sub-conscious mind have a major role in your soul being upgraded or downgraded during the Activation process. At the heart of the activation process are the agreements that you make. Agreements happen during steps 1 (hearing and thinking) and 2 (receiving and believing) of the Activation process. Agreements are powerful.

You can make good agreements or you can make wrong agreements. When an agreement is firmly established through the Activation process, it forms an attachment to your soul. Obviously, you want to form good attachments to your soul that reflect your true identity and renounce wrong attachments which the writer of Hebrews calls a "weight" or a wrong perception.

Let's learn now how agreements work and attachments are formed. (The beginning of this chapter is a little heavy, but hang with us. We are not trying to make your brain hurt. Honest!)

Agreements and Your Sub-Conscious Mind

Your conscious mind receives input from spoken words by you and from other sources such as family members, work associates, the world system, the devil, and from the Spirit of God.

Life-Giving Agreements. When your conscious mind thinks about your identity in a way that is true ("I'm righteous in Christ.") and you think and talk (activation step 3 – speaking) about yourself positively, you make an agreement that aligns with your true identity. We call this agreement a life-giving agreement.

This agreement sends a signal to your sub-conscious mind to dissolve any previous neuropath and begins to build a new, positive path. It causes a recoding/recircuiting of your brain physically to align with your true identity. Then, this agreement forms a new attachment to your soul and causes an upgrade to your identity, and you release and experience the life and peace of God.

- You think and say out loud, "I am well-pleasing to God." Your conscious mind sends this positive agreement to your sub-conscious mind which rewires your brain neuropaths to make it happen. This results in a life-giving attachment to your soul. This contributes to your *I AM Factor*.

Death-Yielding Agreements. Conversely, when your conscious mind thinks and you speak about your identity in a way that is not true ("God is not pleased with me."), you are making an agreement with your *I AM Imposter* (i.e., mistakes, labels from others, lies, negative self-talk). This a "weight" or a wrong perception. This agreement is a death-yielding agreement. Life and death are in the power of your words (Prov. 18:21).

This negative agreement sends a signal to your sub-conscious mind and begins to build a negative neuropath. Your brain is recoding/recircuiting your mind to make that inaccurate view happen. This agreement results in a downgrading in your identity and cuts off the supernatural flow of life from your spirit. This rewiring results in a negative attachment to your soul.

- You think and say aloud, "God is not pleased with me." Your conscious mind sends this negative agreement to your sub-conscious mind which rewires/codes your brain neuropaths to make it happen. You are making a death-yielding attachment to your soul. This contributes to your *I AM Imposter*, your false identity.

To summarize, your conscious mind sends a signal to your sub-conscious mind to recircuit the neuropaths of your physical brain in a new way, either positively or negatively. Your sub-conscious mind takes its cues from your conscious mind. It either upgrades your identity or downgrades it.

Be very aware of what your mind dwells on (and you open your activating valve to), as it is always sending signals to your sub-conscious mind to recircuit neuropaths. Your mind will create thoughts with or without your permission. It can be your master or your servant. Some thoughts you create intentionally and are aware of (in your conscious mind), but most of us are victims of the thoughts created by our subconscious mind.

Your spoken words, and those of others, impact your conscious mind and your subconscious mind takes cues from it. You may not realize that your thoughts and spoken words influence your sub-conscious mind which, in turn, impacts your physical body (emotions, the demeanor you display, posture, etc.).

Here, we are not trying to go deep into how your mind affects your physical brain. Much has been written elsewhere on the connection of the mind to mental health and to physical health. But you need to be aware of the power of your sub-conscious mind to recircuit neuropaths that either upgrade or downgrade your life.

Let's take a brief look at the architecture of the mind.

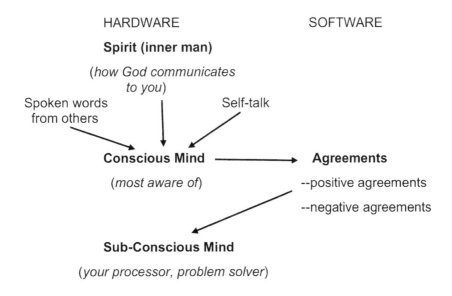

Architecture of the Mind

Think of your **hardware** as the component parts of your inner self: your spirit man, conscious mind (what you are most aware of), and sub-conscious mind (your processor, problem solver).

- The words you receive (from your spirit, from others, your self-talk) affect your conscious mind which, in turn, impacts words you speak; your words feed your sub-conscious mind.

- Your sub-conscious mind has no filter; it looks for something to do and problems to solve (whether you give it permission to do so or not). Your sub-conscious mind takes its lead from your conscious mind.

- Your born-again spirit (how God communicates with you) greatly influences both your conscious and sub-conscious mind.

Your **software** consists of the positive and negative contracts or agreements you make with something. When you agree with something, your sub-conscious mind begins to code or rewire the neuropaths to make the agreement happen.

Speaking words is a part of the Activation process. Each time we speak words about ourselves, our lives, and our future, we affect the direction and working of our minds.

The Activation process includes relearning and recircuiting. Recall, the heart of our Father views us as learners, and not failures. He only works from our new nature, our new self in Christ. Activation involves relearning, rethinking, repenting, ridding ourselves of inaccurate understandings of our identity, and receiving an upgraded identity. We need to be upgraded in our identity for each season we are in.

So, how can you rewire your agreements so your neuropaths align with your true identity?

Rewiring Our Agreements

Let's look at the process of rewiring the agreements we make with our words, because our words impact our thinking (conscious and sub-conscious), our attitudes, and actions.

With your words, you plant or sow into the spiritual realm as well as the natural realm including your sub-conscious mind, which also impacts your physical brain. You plant and sow with your words.

> *I have put My words in your mouth. . . . that I may plant the heavens.* Is. 51:16 NKJV

Regarding your identity in Christ, you are speaking and sowing words that either upgrade your identity releasing the life of God, or words that downgrade your identity releasing death; death and life are in the power of the tongue (Prov. 18:21).

God is seeking to plant His words about your true identity into your mind and heart, and you need to partner with Him and speak what He sees when He looks at you.

The **words** you speak and plant affect your **thoughts and feelings**, which in turn impact your **actions** and ultimately the **results** (i.e. success, failure, beliefs about self, about God, etc.). This is a continuous cycle.

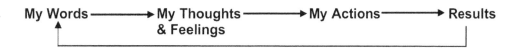

Recircuiting is a Putting Off and a Putting On

Recircuiting occurs during the Activation process as a *putting off* and a *putting on*.

Let's revisit Ephesians 4:22-25:

> . . .<u>lay aside</u> the old self. . . and that you be <u>renewed</u> in the spirit of your mind, and <u>put on</u> the new self, which in the likeness of God has been created in righteousness and holiness of the truth. Therefore, <u>laying aside</u> falsehood [pseudo], <u>speak truth.</u> . .

These are important elements of the recircuiting process.

PUT OFF the imposter: Put off or lay aside the falsehood (*pseudos* = lies, imposter, fake) notions of who you are. This means to *renounce* and *reject* them as not who you are. This is the repenting phase.

- Actively renounce and reject, and cut all ties with each false notion. Put them to death.
- Root out entrenched habits (i.e., critical words, quick to anger, tendency to be fearful).

If you have a deep-seated wound in your spirit from a prior experience that resulted in a vivid negative memory, you will need to *aggressively* root out that memory and feel it and replace it with the truth about your identity in Christ. This can be especially challenging if there is a strong emotional attachment associated with that memory.

Put off wrong hearing – labels, lies.
Put off wrong believing, feelings and attitudes.
Put off wrong speaking – negative self-talk.
Put off wrong habits and practices.

In doing so, you are removing inaccurate perceptions, wrong beliefs, agreements, and attachments from your soul.

Your mistakes, labels from others, wrong attitudes, and negative self-talk do not belong to you. Jesus paid dearly for them, therefore, they don't belong to you. They belong to Jesus, so put off these things and give them back to Jesus. He crucified and buried them for you, and He did not bring them through the resurrection. He only resurrected your new self in newness of life. Consider yourself dead to these negative things. Be careful of the agreements that you agree to and speak.

> Your mistakes, labels from others, wrong attitudes, and negative self-talk do not belong to you... They belong to Jesus.

The Father only sees one version of you – your new man. He killed off your old self at the cross.

RENEW: To renew means to relearn. Actively renew your mind with the truth of who you are in your born-again spirit as found in the Word of God. You are implanting the truth into your mind.

PUT ON more of Your New Self: Speak out-loud what is true about you and the life within you. In faith, actively *announce*, *confess*, and *embrace* out-loud the truth about your identity in Christ. This is like *receiving* and being *fully clothed* with a new garment. As you do, the Father is upgrading you on the inside, taking you up higher into your identity.

Put on right hearing – based on your true identity in Christ.
Put on right believing and attitudes.
Put on right speaking – positive self-talk.
Put on right habits and righteous lifestyle.

Now, you are believing right and making good agreements and attachments to your soul.

Let's Ponder!

What are those things in your mind that you need to reject, renounce, and cut out?

What do you need to "put to death?"

What are some ways that you can form the new man in your mind and heart?

The Recircuiting Steps

The first step is DIAGNOSIS and it begins with a God Talk[6]. Ask the Lord two questions about lies and truths about your identity. Take the time to listen to what the Lord says to you and write them down.

> What **lies** do I believe about my identity that I need to change?

> What's **true** about my identity?

Once you have answers and scriptures from the Lord, move on to the final step: the CURE.

---

[6] Ed Rush, **God Talks** handout, https://edrush.com/wp-content/uploads/2022/04/God-Talks-Event-Handout.pdf, downloaded November 15, 2022

For each lie about your true identity, you must repent, reject and renounce and then declare or announce what is really true from scripture. In so doing, you are making a new agreement.

DIAGNOSIS	CURE / REWIRING
Ask God 2 questions:	*(making new neuro-connections)*
What **LIES** do I believe about [my identity]? (failure, disappointed God, feel unworthy, etc.)	I **reject and renounce** the lie that _____.
What's **TRUE** about [my identity]? (success, God is proud of me, not disappointed in me)	I choose to believe and **declare and announce** that _____.
	(making new agreements)

Recircuiting Steps

Now, you have made a new agreement with your conscious mind and in faith you speak words of the new agreement into the spiritual realm and the physical realm. This sends a signal to your sub-conscious mind which begins to dissolve the negative neuropath and begins to build the new neuropath. Choose to make only positive agreements with your words and mind.

This process physically recodes or rewires your brain.

To summarize, with the words of your new agreement, you are partnering with God to recode your thinking and feelings, which drives your actions, which drives the new result (beliefs about you, God, your future, etc.).

In our journey, we had wrong thoughts to renounce and replace with the truth about God's heart toward us. We wanted to know that we belonged to Him. We began to rewire our thinking about the Father's heart toward us and declaring such truths as:

- I am totally accepted by God (Rom. 15:7; Eph. 1:5-6 NKJV)
- I am well pleasing to God because I am in Christ Who was well-pleasing to the Father (Matt. 3:17; Mark 1:11)
- I am approved (I Thess. 2:4)
- I am chosen by God, holy and dearly loved (Col. 3:12; I Pet. 2:9)

Let's Ponder!

Have a God Talk:

What lies do you believe about yourself? What is true about you?

What lies do you believe about God? What is true about God?

What lies do you believe about your past? What is true about your past?

What lies do you believe about your future? What is true about your future?

What lies do you believe about your purpose? What is true about your purpose?

Examples

Let's look at three examples of the recircuiting steps in action. Notice that every **inaccurate perception** has a **promise/truth** (a correct perception from scripture) with a **provision** attached to it. Declare only who you really are.

From *I Feel Rejected. . .* to *God Deeply Loves and Totally Accepts Me!*

Romans 15:7

Therefore, accept one another, just as Christ also accepted us to the glory of God.

Romans 5:5

The love of God has been poured out within our hearts through the Holy Spirit who was given to us.

I REPENT and RENOUNCE the lie that I am rejected, and ANNOUNCE the truth that God deeply loves me and He totally accepts me!

I declare that I am deeply loved by God!

I declare that I am totally accepted and fully pleasing to God!

From *I Feel Depressed*. . . to *God Has Provided Me with <u>Peace</u> and <u>Joy</u>!*

Philippians 4:4

Rejoice in the Lord always; again I will say, rejoice!

Philippians 4:7

And the peace of God, which surpasses all comprehension, will guard your hearts and your minds in Christ Jesus.

Romans 15:13

Now may the God of hope fill you with all joy and peace in believing, so that you will abound in hope by the power of the Holy Spirit.

I REPENT and RENOUNCE all feelings of depression, and ANNOUNCE the truth that God has provided me with peace and joy!

I declare that I will rejoice in the Lord continually!

I declare that I choose to live a life filled with joy!

I declare that I have the peace of God which passes all understanding!

From *My Future Seems Bleak*. . . to *God Has a Great Plan for My Life!*

Psalm 139:14, 16

I am fearfully and wonderfully made.

In Your book were all written the days that were ordained for me.

Jeremiah 29:11, 13

'For I know the plans that I have for you,' declares the Lord, 'plans for welfare and not for calamity to give you a future and a hope.' You will seek Me and find Me when you search for Me with all your heart.

Acts 13:36

For David. . . served the purpose of God in his own generation.

I REPENT and RENOUNCE the lie that God has a bleak future for me, and ANNOUNCE the truth that God is absolutely good and has a great plan and destiny for my life!

I declare that my destiny that You have written in Your destiny book about me in heaven will come to pass!

I choose to connect to my destiny!

I declare that Father God is absolutely good and has a good plan for my life!

I decree that I will fulfill my God-given destiny and assignment in this season!

I decree that I will serve and fulfill the purposes of God in my generation!

I declare that I am a leader who is taking my place in the King's Ekklesia!

Let's Internalize and Apply!

1. What are the three items of the 'hardware' part of our mind?

   _____

   _____

   _____

2. What is the 'software' part of our mind?

   _____

   _____

   _____

3. What is the effect of an agreement on your sub-conscious mind?

   _____

   _____

   _____

4. What are the two types of agreements?

   _____

   _____

   _____

5. In the Recircuiting steps, what are the two questions to ask the Lord in the Diagnosis step?

_____

_____

_____

6. What are the two phases of the Cure (or Rewiring) step?

_____

_____

_____

Chapter 15

"Give Me Back My Stuff!"

"Let us lay aside [renounce] *every weight,* [wrong perception] *and the sin which so easily ensnares us. (*Heb. 12:1 NKJV, brackets added)

We have grown up in a world that is pretty negative. Negatives include such things as anxiety and worry, fear, anger, doubt and unbelief, and frustration.

The world is inherently negative but the Kingdom isn't. Negatives are those things which are not a part of your new nature in Christ or the fruit of the Spirit. Negatives are a wrong perception about who you are, and not how heaven perceives or views you. All negativity wars against your identity in Christ, against your sonship in Christ. There are no negatives, wrong perceptions, or frustrations in heaven.

Negativity and negative self-talk do not belong to you; they are not a part of your new man in Christ. Jesus paid dearly for them, therefore, they don't belong to you. They belong to Jesus, so put off these things and give them back to Jesus. He crucified and buried them for you, and He did not bring them through the resurrection. He only resurrected your new self in newness of life. Consider yourself dead to these negative things and remove them from your soul. Be careful of the agreements that you agree to and speak.

The Duck and the Sponge

We each respond to negativity in different ways in differing situations. But we seem to have a propensity to respond in one of two ways.

You may be a person who tends to be a **sponge** as you respond to negativity. For example, someone may say something negative about you. As a sponge soaks up water, you respond by absorbing the negative thought and negative feeling associated with the negative comment. If you don't squeeze out the negative thought and feeling, you begin to adopt it as a part of your identity and act accordingly.

Or, you may be a person who generally responds to negativity like a **duck**. You don't seem to let negative thoughts bother you, as you let the thought and feeling associated with the negative comment "run off like water off a duck's back."

Laurie speaking: *I have a melancholy temperament so I tend to absorb feelings of negativity like a sponge pretty easily. When I hear a negative statement made, I often absorb the feeling and the thinking that goes with it. Lon not so much, as he tends to respond to negativity like a duck. He doesn't seem to let negative thoughts bother him very much as he typically will not accept those words or feelings.*

Let's Ponder!

When it comes to responding to negativity, do you tend to respond like a sponge or like a duck?

Jesus Said, "Give Me Back My Stuff!"

I want to share a dream that Graham Cook shared about being caught up to heaven.[7]

Graham said that he had similar dreams as this one where Jesus was marching up with a smile on His face and was hugging others along the way. This time, Jesus was marching up the hill looking annoyed.

Jesus: *"Give me back my stuff!"*

Graham: "I don't know what you mean, Lord."

---

[7] Graham Cooke, *Jesus Demanded Graham Cooke, "Give Me Back My Stuff,"* https://www.youtube.com/watch?v=A-dBioGxk0E, July 7, 2014

Jesus: *"Graham, don't mess with me. Give me back my stuff!"*

Graham: "I don't know what you mean."

Jesus: *"Sure you do. Give me back my stuff! I want it. And I want it right now!"*

Graham: "Jesus, I gave you everything. Honest."

Jesus: *"You took some stuff from me and I don't want you to have it. Now give it back to me."*

Graham: "I really don't know what you mean Lord."

Jesus: *"This is the last time. Give me back my stuff."*

Graham: "What stuff?"

Jesus: *"All that worry, that anger, that resentment, bitterness, fear. I died for it. I paid a price for it. It belongs to me. It doesn't belong to you. Give me back my stuff!"*

Graham: "Oh my God, I now get it. All those things You died for, You took them to the cross, and I've been resurrecting them. And I'm utterly appalled. I'm so sorry."

Jesus picked me up, pulled me up to Him, and smiled. (I felt like I was getting saved all over again!).

Jesus: *"Have you any idea how delighted I was to die for all those things? When I was on the cross, it was the joy that was set before Me to die for all those things. On the cross, I knew that I was robbing you of experiencing all that negativity. I was taking all those things so that you would never have to experience them ever again. I could give you a whole new life where all those things are absent.*

You need to learn a different way of being.

Do you know how excited I was to take all those things away from you – to never be fearful again, or worried or panicked? To never have to be angry, or bitter or resentful? To never have to do any of that stuff again? You can be free of all negativity.

All your negative ways of looking at things that make you cynical and sarcastic. All your negative ways of seeing or thinking. Ways that make you imagine the worst before seeing the best – that takes you into the shadows, the darkness where you imagine and think the worst."

"I robbed you of all that negativity so you can <u>see</u> the best, <u>think</u> the best, <u>believe</u> the best, and <u>be</u> the best."

"And you keep taking it all back, like it belongs to you. It doesn't belong to you. I died for it. I paid a price for it. It's mine. Give Me back my stuff. You can't have it."

"All the time you are taking hold of these things, you can't see who you really are. You can't be the person I see when I look at you. Every time you take up all those things, this is a disconnect between you and heaven. I died so that you could stay connected. It's called, abiding – staying, remaining in that place in Me."

"Graham, I want my stuff back! As long as you hold on to all those things, you actually cannot receive all the things I want to give you. I can only give to you in exchange for all that stuff. Then you can have My accelerated goodness, My grace, My power."

"Son, give me back my stuff. You and I have important things to do."

End of dream.

When Graham awoke from the dream, he said he wrote down all the things he had taken from Jesus. Next to those things he wrote all the positive things that were the opposite of those negative things. He turned each negative into a positive. Does this sound like the Recircuiting steps in chapter 14 – renouncing and then announcing?

Jesus continued to instruct him: *"Stop defaulting to your old man, your old nature which is dead, instead of developing and responding with the fruit of the Spirit. I'm dealt with your sin at the Cross and now I'm dealing with holiness – so I deal with your negativity.*

"Every time you get into these situations, you always default to the old man which is dead. When you take stuff back from Me, you default back to the old man that has already been killed off. You aren't living in your true identity."

Making War on Negativity

Negativity is not a part of your identity in Christ.

Every negative, whether anxiety, worry, fear, doubt, or frustration, becomes a weight that hinders the free manifestation of your true identity in Christ (Heb. 12:1). You are to lay aside every weight, all negativity which so easily entangles you. Negatives are not your true identity in Christ.

- All negativity is an assault against your identity in Christ.
- Negatives distract you from your true identity and destiny.
- Negatives can distort how you perceive who you really are in Christ.
- Negatives challenge the truths God has declared about you

> *All negativity is an assault against your identity in Christ.*

Negativity leads to wrong perceptions about God and about yourself, and manifests as negative behavior, negative thinking, negative emotions, sarcasm, and cynicism.

The Holy Spirit exposes the lies of negativity regarding your true identity and wants to correct how you see yourself, think about yourself, and talk about yourself.

All your negatives have already been addressed at the Cross.

Here's the good news! All negatives were crucified and buried in Christ with our sins. Negativity is a part of the old man, not the new man.

The shed blood of Christ has already paid for all negatives in your life. They don't belong to you. Our perspective needs to be:

> If it doesn't exist in heaven, it can't exist here.
> If it is not intended, then don't allow it.
> If it is not in Christ, you don't want it. Don't accept it.

A negative is a weight that was crucified and buried in Christ along with your sins. Let your sin and all negativity, buried with Christ, rest in peace in the grave.

When you are weary and heavy-laden — with all your negative attachments, negative thinking, negative emotions — Jesus directs you to come to Him and give Him your negatives. He will give you rest. He invites you to take His yoke and learn from Him (Matt. 11:28-30). When you do, His yoke is easy and light because there are no negatives attached to it. Consider yourself dead to all negativity and give it back to Jesus. His yoke does not contain any negativity.

Negativity presses against your born-again spirit and your walk in the Spirit.

Negatives press against your walk in the Spirit and the full expression of the fruit of the Spirit. The lies of all negatives press against and challenge:

- your perception of what's true in your born-again spirit, (which is as righteous, complete, and perfect as Jesus is now)
- how you think and feel about yourself, and
- how you talk about yourself.

Negatives will seek to restrict, frustrate, or even nullify the flow of God's grace in your life (Gal. 2:21). Since you are crucified with Christ, and your old nature is in the grave, don't let negativity frustrate the flow of the grace of God in your life.

Think of a negative as an *attachment* (a weight) to a way of life that is taught by the flesh, the world and religion. It seeks to portray the Lord but can never produce His fullness of life in you (see the illustration below). A negative can become a behavior pattern, a way of thinking or feeling that is unhelpful. The solution is to convert negatives into an upgrade of true identity in Christ.

> A negative can become a behavior pattern, a way of thinking or feeling that is unhelpful.

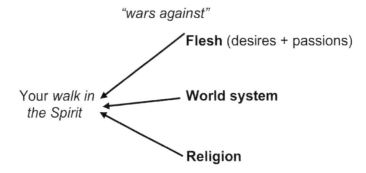

Check out these scriptures which describe this 'warring against' your identity in Christ.

Flesh

Walk by the Spirit, and you will not carry out the desire of the flesh. For <u>the flesh</u> sets its desire <u>against the Spirit</u>, and the Spirit against the flesh; for these are in opposition to one another. . . Those who belong to Christ Jesus have crucified the flesh with its passions and desires. Gal. 5:16-17, 24

For. . .the <u>lust</u> of the <u>flesh</u>. . .is not from the Father. I John 2:16

World system

Do not love the world nor the things in the world. If anyone <u>loves</u> the <u>world</u>, the love of the Father is not in him. I John 2:15

Religion

But if you are led by the Spirit, you are not <u>under the Law</u> [religion]. Galatians 5:18

Remember, religion seeks for you to work on the negative thought using a behavior modification approach (focusing on your old nature) – working from the outside. Religion is what the apostle Paul spoke against in Galatians 3:3:

Having begun by the Spirit, are you now being perfected by the flesh [works, religion]?

The Kingdom never works on a negative (using behavior modification); rather, Holy Spirit works *within* you by prompting you to change that negative thought into a truth about your identity, and works on that thought. God only speaks to you from your identity in Christ.

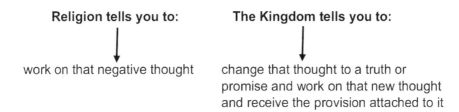

For example, religion tells you to work on your negative thought, say worry. On the other hand, the Kingdom tells you not to think about worry, but to change it into a promise such as, "cast all your anxieties on Him, because He cares for you" (1 Pet. 5:7). Work on that instead and receive the provision of rest attached to it. Give Jesus back your worries – about life, about tomorrow, about what you eat, drink, or wear. These worries don't belong to you.

Negativity, if not addressed, will result in doubt and unbelief (vs. faith), and fear (vs. love). We are to walk by "faith working through love" (Gal. 5:6).

The Lord refuses to work with a negative because there are no negatives in heaven.

Holy Spirit seeks to convert the negative or wrong perception into something that is true about the new man so He can deal with it. The Godhead only works on your new man, never the old.

We often have *negative* thoughts about ourselves. If all your negative thoughts about yourself bring you to a place you don't like, have a better thought by rewiring your agreements! Clearly, that thought is not working for you!

Rather, we partner with Holy Spirit to convert a negative into a positive truth about your identity in Christ through the Recircuiting steps:

- Rejecting/Renouncing the negative agreement, and
- Announcing/Declaring the truth about your identity in Christ, making new agreements and attachments.

Once you rewire your thinking according to the new man in Christ, your identity in Christ becomes upgraded in your heart and mind. As you have learned, declaring audibly out-loud impacts the spiritual realm as well as your subconscious mind.

In our journey to be upgraded in our identity, we discovered that who we are falls into three categories: the I AM truths, the I HAVE truths, and the I CAN DO truths. A listing of the truths for the last two are found in Appendices D and E.

In addition, the I AM truths seem to fall into three clusters: I am Accepted, I am Secure, and I am Significant. A listing of these truths are found in Appendices A, B, and C. The activating prayers for the truths in each cluster are found in chapters 19, 20, and 21 respectively.

Diagnosis and Cure Revisited

Lon speaking: *Periodically I have times when the Lord reveals wrong perceptions and lies in my thinking and the words I speak about who I am. I choose to apply the two questions from the previous chapter to **diagnose** the lie and then replace it with the **cure** – the truth about me. Below are the major areas which I needed to rewire (recircuit) in my mind and my words. I countered with these truths:*

- I am completely forgiven of all of my sins – past, present, and future (I John 2:1-2; Heb. 9:12, 15; 10:10, 14)
- I am free from condemnation because Jesus has given me the gift of no-condemnation (Rom. 8:1, 34).
- I am fully qualified to share in the fullness of His inheritance (Col. 1:12).
- I am well pleasing to God because I am in Christ Who was well-pleasing to the Father (Matt. 3:17; Mark 1:11)
- I am righteous (Eph. 4:24; II Cor. 5:21); that is, I am the righteousness of God in Christ Jesus.
- I am perfect, complete, and mature (Heb. 10:14; 12:23)
- I am a victor, not a victim. I have the victory through the Lord Jesus Christ (I Cor. 15:57)

Let's Ponder!

Returning to the two question to ask God:

*What are the **lies**, wrong perceptions, and negativity that I have believed and agreed to that need to be renounced and rejected?*

*What is the **truth** about my identity that I need to embrace and declare that results in a new agreement and attachment?*

So, there is a new version of you that the Holy Spirit is working with. When Holy Spirit is pointing something out in your life that isn't working, He points to the site of your *next* upgrade, the site of your next miracle. When Holy Spirit shines the light on a lie that is a negative in your life, He says, "This is brilliant, let's get to work on that next!"

Remember, your old man is dead and therefore you don't have a sin nature anymore. However, the problem we often have is that we yield to a negative or a temptation and **default** to our old nature that is dead in the grave. Defaulting to your old nature (having a *sin consciousness*) seeks to resurrect your old nature (that Christ already killed off and buried in the grave). Instead, be reminded that you are developing a *righteousness consciousness* of yourself.

We all have areas in our life that need renovation. God makes us complete in Christ (Col. 1:28) and also allows us to grow into completion. This means: God gives you everything up front and then teaches you how to stay full. You are complete in Him and He teaches you what that completeness looks like. So everything in your life is brilliantly positive. When God looks at you, He sees you in Christ and He says, "Yes and Amen."

Let's partner with Holy Spirit and give Jesus back His stuff!

Let's Ponder!

God is asking: I'm making war with all your wrong perceptions and negativity. Will you partner with Me to recircuit and activate your true identity and the fruit of the Spirit?

What are some ways that you can make war on your negativity and wrong perceptions using love, grace, patience, joy, peace, and mercy?

What negative thoughts are holding you back?

Let's Internalize and Apply!

1. T/F All negativity is at war against your identity or sonship in Christ. _____

2. Are negativity and negative self-talk a part of your new man in Christ?

   _____

   _____

   _____

3. When Jesus says to give Him back His stuff, what does He want returned?

   _____

   _____

   _____

4. How can you use the Recircuiting steps from the previous chapter to exchange negativity for truth?

5. In what four ways does negativity war against your true identity in Christ?

6. In what three areas does negativity press against your born-again spirit?

7. Negativity can be thought of as an attachment or weight to your life that comes from what three sources?

8. What does the kingdom of God tell you to focus on regarding a negative thought? How does this differ from what religion tells you to do?

_____

_____

_____

9. T/F The Lord refuses to work with a negative because there are no negatives in heaven. _____

Chapter 16

Taking Down Your Giants

And do not be conformed to this world [default to the old man], *but be transformed* [upgraded] *by the renewing of your mind* [to the new man]. (Romans 12:2, brackets added)

Every negative thing around you is designed to give you an upgrade. So you may need a new perspective and way of thinking about how God wants to use circumstances as a means to upgrade your identity.

Circumstances, problems, and wrong perceptions are all opportunities for the Lord to upgrade your identity in Him – who you are in Him.

When Jesus died on the cross and God put all of your sins on Him, He also put all of your negative behavior, negative thinking, negative emotions, sarcasm, and cynicism on the cross too.

You need not talk or think negatively about anything. Why would you want to — because there is a way of thinking in Jesus that is stunning. Every obstacle is designed to elevate you!

When you encounter an obstacle (at work, at home, in life, etc.), you may choose to be frustrated out of default to the old man, when you could be upgraded to the new man – which is who you really are in Christ. Your soul needs to catch up with what has already transpired in your new man.

> When Jesus died on the cross and God put all of your sins on Him, He also put all of your negative behavior, negative thinking, negative emotions, sarcasm, and cynicism on the cross too.

Too often, however, we default to the world system around us — to the culture we grew up in, to religious traditions — when in reality God is seeking to elevate us using a different way of thinking. God is going to change you to be like Him, which means he is going to totally change the way you think.

Here's the thing: *God doesn't want to think like you. He doesn't want to be made in your image.* There is a reason He killed off the old man – your old nature. He wanted to make you brand new, stunning, and brilliant like Jesus, so consider yourself dead to the old man and alive to the new man.

Consider yourself dead to all negativity and alive unto God!

Giants Upgrade You

God uses giants in your life to upgrade you.

There are always giants in the land. There is always a giant next to a promise because you need a giant to upgrade your identity in Him. Remember, the Lord is continually upgrading you in (1) your identity, (2) the fruit of the Spirit being formed in you, and (3) who God is and wants to be for you (introduced in chapter two).

> Isn't it just like God to put a giant next to a promise because you need a giant to upgrade your identity in Him.

God says to you:

"Do you see that giant? The size of that giant is what I am making you into. In the conflict, We are going to make you that size, and the giant is going to become your present size. The giant against you has to be bigger and stronger than you because of what you are becoming. The giant is your doorway into your new place of strength."

Caleb and Joshua: In Numbers 13 and 14, Caleb was one of the 12 spies sent out by Moses to spy out the Promised Land. All 12 men were champions and warriors, but 10 of the spies saw themselves as grasshoppers (a diminished, downgraded view of their identity). Caleb, along with Joshua, came back bigger than when they went out and saw themselves as powerful as the giants: "*The Lord is with us. . . for they will be our prey*" (Num. 14:9). Caleb came back with an upgraded identity, which gave him a majesty mindset. His faith was greatly upgraded!

David. In I Samuel 17, David had been upgraded by both the lion and the bear (v. 36), and God was using the giant Goliath to give David another upgrade in his identity and save the nation of Israel.

What did Caleb, Joshua, and David have in common? They each faced giants.

When God shows you a giant, He is saying, "That is the size I am making you into." You need to be that big because the weight of promise and destiny on your life is much bigger than you can handle where you are right now. So you need a promised land with giants in it to strengthen you and upgrade you to carry the weight of favor that actually belongs to you.

When the Lord allows a giant to come our way to upgrade us, we tend to ask the wrong questions:

"Lord, why am I going through this?" (the WHY question)

"Lord, when will this be over?" (the WHEN question)

Giant killers don't ask the WHY and WHEN questions, they ask the WHAT question followed by the HOW question:

*"Lord, **what** do You want me to become as I take down this giant?"*

*"**What** do You need to change in me so I can be upgraded and conquer this giant?"*

*"**What** does God want to be for me in this moment to make me the size of the giant?"*

*"Lord, **how** can I partner with you to receive the upgrade You want to give me?"*

Don't ask the "Why" question. Why me? Why now? Why this? Because the why question seldom gets answered on earth. It's an invalid question that makes you an *invalid* if you ask it. It's a victim question.

Holy Spirit is training you to see things as He sees them. This is your birthright in Jesus.

So don't be in fear of their size, weapons, or mockery. May we instead run toward them and be upgraded in the process.

> Don't ask the "Why" question. Because the why question seldom gets answered on earth. It's an *invalid* question that makes you an *invalid* if you ask it. It's a victim question.

Laurie speaking: *Even though I was a victim of an automobile accident, Lon and I were determined not let this giant of an experience cause us to see ourselves as victims. Our motto was and still is: "I am a victor, not a victim." In terms of standing and walking, I was a physical invalid for a number of months. But I believed that condition was temporary and that I would walk normally once again. Thank God I can stand and walk normally again! I am now able to go for one-to two-mile walks with Lon.*

Periodically through our journey, we did ask the WHY and the WHEN questions, but we did not camp there. We tried to stay focused on the WHAT questions, receiving His abundant grace each day through the many months, followed by the HOW questions. His grace was rich and it upgraded us for the next season of our life.

Lon speaking: *We realized early in this situation that we needed to be teachable and draw close to the Lord and listen to His voice. As we did, the Lord led us to focus on who we were in Him – our identity – and to be open to who He wanted to be for us. We were learning a relationship of dependence on the Holy Spirit. This giant of an experience resulted in a transition from an attitude of independence ("We can do this ourselves") to an attitude of dependence ("Holy Spirit, help us live daily in partnership with you"). We were being upgraded in our identity not only for that season of our lives but for the next season.*

Let's Ponder!

How can you adopt a mindset that giants in your life are there to upgrade your identity in Him?

What giants are in your life now that God wants to use to give you an upgraded identity for the season you are in?

What negative is God putting His finger on in your life to upgrade and give you a majesty mindset – so you become the head and not the tail?

Taking Down Your Giants

Giant killers make choices from their *identity* and not from their *circumstances*.

Make choices from your *identity* rather than your *circumstances*. A giant killer first figures out who they are and who they can be in the moment.

Most people come to God first with their circumstances, rather than engage God with their own *character* and *identity*. They don't allow the circumstances to initiate an upgrade in their identity. Rather, they just want God to change the circumstances they are going through at the moment.

Every situation in life is designed to make you more like Jesus. Rather than asking God to rescue us from our circumstances, start focusing on God's majesty and supremacy in all things. The Father has never been overwhelmed by anything. Jesus is undefeated and the Holy Spirit always leads us to triumph (2 Cor. 2:14). You are triumphant!

Make it a practice to approach your circumstances as an opportunity for the Lord to upgrade your identity in Him. If you don't approach choices this way, you are going to have this circumstance come around again and again! How many times have you had this situation in the last 8 – 10 years?

Giant killers know that when they understand the process of upgrading their identity, it puts them in a position above the circumstance, not below it. They focus on their new man identity in Christ.

> The Father has never been overwhelmed by anything. Jesus is undefeated and the Holy Spirit always leads us to triumph. You are triumphant!

Without an upgrade in your identity and standing, you will not be equipped or ready to work on your new assignment. God is calling us higher – to spiral upward and forward in Him. He takes us to the next level.

You need an upgraded identity that matches and conquers the giants awaiting you at the next level. The weight of promise and destiny on your life requires you to be much bigger than you are right now. Without this upgrade, you aren't equipped to go to the next level. God is likely using a giant or two in your life right now to upgrade and elevate you for the next season.

The next season may be a new ministry with expanded responsibilities, a promoted position in your company, or a new leadership position in an organization.

Living in Your Standing (Identity) in Christ

You are to live in your standing in Jesus, not in your situation.

We tend to focus first on our **situation**, which is how our old man would see our circumstance, with a default to the negative. (WHEN will this be over? WHY is this taking so long?)

When you approach with your **standing**, you think and speak from your new man in Christ — about who God is for you, what you are learning, who you are becoming. You ask the WHAT and HOW questions: What do you want me to learn? How do You want me to be upgraded?

God addresses your standing or identity before He addresses your situation. He does this in two phases.

Phase 1: God upgrades the *standing* in your spirit man to give you an upgraded identity. This updated identity is "who you are becoming." Your new man in Christ makes all the difference as you take an upgrade standing into your situations.

Phase 2: You partner with the Lord to take your updated identity into your situation and transform that situation.

> If you are in Christ, and seated with Him in heaven, so are all of your circumstances. So they have to line up with His purposes.

If you are in Christ, and seated with Him in heaven, so are all of your circumstances. The Presence of God is vital because you can put your circumstances in His Presence too. When you put your circumstances into Christ, they have to line up with His purposes.

Your first priority should be seeking a relational upgrade with the Lord. Then, take that upgrade in relationship and release it along with the Presence of God into your circumstances.

Giant killers live in Christ, not in their circumstances. They are like Caleb, a person of a different sort seeking to be like Jesus.

God wants to upgrade you by increasing your revelation of who Jesus is for you. He wants to accelerate the development of the fruit of the Spirit in your life to transform your situation. Jesus wants to baptize you in the Holy Spirit so you can receive the spiritual resources you need for your next assignment. And, we wants to make your spiritual gifts operational to take you to the next level.

Make these decisions today:

1. Always live in Jesus and not in the situation. If you are in Christ, so are all of your circumstances.

2. Separate your identity in Christ from your situation to make sure you receive a true upgrade.

3. Then, lead with your upgraded identity along with Jesus into your circumstances, and become what He wants you to become and act the way He wants you to act.

As you do, you will profit from whatever is going on in your life. You need to be around like-minded people because they elevate you. You sharpen one another.

Let your giants upgrade you.

Activating Your True Identity

Let's Internalize and Apply!

1. T/F. On the cross, Jesus died not only for your sins but also your negative behavior, negative thinking, negative emotions, sarcasm, and cynicism. _____

2. What three areas is the Lord continually upgrading in you?

   _____

   _____

   _____

3. When God shows you a giant to conquer, what is He saying to you?

   _____

   _____

   _____

4. What are the two wrong questions we often ask?

   _____

   _____

   _____

5. What are the two questions we should be asking instead?

   _____

   _____

   _____

6. There is a difference between your standing and your situation. Which one does God want to address and upgrade first?

   _____

   _____

   _____

7. T/F Giant killers live in Christ and lead with their upgraded identity and Jesus into their circumstance. _____

Chapter 17

A Soul That Prospers

Let us lay aside [renounce] every weight [negativity], and the sin which so easily ensnares us. . .
(Hebrews 12:1, NKJV, brackets added)

Beloved, I pray that in all respects you may prosper and be in good health, just as your soul prospers.
(3 John 2)

This is the season for the sons and daughters of God to shine. To be powerful in this season requires that you prosper in your soul because out of your heart flows the springs of life (Prov. 4:23). A soul that is clean and pure and unencumbered from negativity allows you to prosper in your health, your finances, your ministry, and to succeed in all of life.

> **Negative attachments. . . press against and diminish the full expression of your true identity in Christ.**

We often allow unhelpful things to attach to our soul which can become locked-in as habits. This occurs when we make negative agreements. These weights often become an *attachment* to a way of life taught by the world, the flesh and religion that seeks to distort our view of self and of God. Negative attachments can never produce His fullness of life in us but rather press against and diminish the full expression of our true identity in Christ.

The instruction from scripture is: *Lay aside [renounce] every weight [negativity] and the sin which so easily entangles us. . .so that your soul prospers [thrives].*

So how can you cleanse your soul when it has become weighed down with worries, negative thinking and feelings, and wrong habits? How can you return to a place of having a clean and prosperous soul that thrives and reflects what is true about your born-again spirit — your true identity?

Previously, we learned the four steps of Activation: hearing the word, believing the word, speaking the word, and finally doing the word and putting it into action. Then, we went deeper into Activation when we learned the recircuiting process to rewire your conscious mind and sub-conscious mind: Rejecting and renouncing the lie and announcing and declaring the truth about your soul. Recircuiting is a putting off and a putting on. Let's learn another practical tool of putting off and putting on.

Doing a Soul Check-Up[8]

Negatives are a habit, a behavior pattern, a way of thinking that is unhelpful. Negative attachments and habits can be redeemed and broken with a 2-step process: loosing from our soul, and binding to our soul.

Jesus said:

> *I will build My church* [ecclesia]*. . . I will give you the keys of the kingdom of heaven; and whatever you bind on earth shall have been bound in heaven, and whatever you loose on earth shall have been loosed in heaven. (*Matthew 16:18-19, bracket added)

Ecclesia, the Greek word translated, "church", is a government term, and not a religious term. The ecclesia was the governing authority in the region whose function was to be God's legislature on the earth. So it should come as no surprise that the word *bind* and the word *loose* are legal or governmental terms – they are legal rulings. You can make a binding agreement; or you can go to court and have a contract or agreement dissolved or loosed.

In chapter 14 we learned that our minds make agreements – some positive and others negative – that result in attachments to our soul. We need to loose these wrong attachments from our soul.

The keys of the Kingdom of *binding* and *loosing* mean we have governmental authority to:

---

[8] Kat Kerr, *Cleansing the Soul Declarations*, https://www.youtube.com/watch?v=Ts38BFFl3i4, downloaded November 15, 2022

Permit or not permit

Allow or not allow

Forbid or not forbid

Tolerate or not tolerate

Accept or not accept

Lock and unlock

Open and close.

Let's now apply this 2-step cleansing process to your soul and keep it unencumbered from negativity.

Step 1: Loosing from Your Soul

Here is the sentence stem to use to release weights and negative attachments from your soul:

I choose with my will to loose from my soul. . . [the negative attachment].

These statements break the negative agreement that you made somewhere along the line. Choose, believe, and speak that which you want released. Here are some sample statements to speak out loud and do business in the spirit realm:

I choose with my will to loose from my soul:

Any unforgiveness, any offense, any hurtful, mean, and unjust accusations against me whether spoken or written. I loose them from my soul in Jesus' Name.

I choose with my will to loose from my soul:

Any curses spoken over me, or any of my family, anywhere in my heritage. I loose those curses right now in Jesus' Name.

I choose with my will to loose from my soul:

Any and all profanity, any curses, and any harsh, critical, mean, hateful, or spiteful words that have been spoken to me. I loose them in Jesus' Name.

I choose with my will to loose from my soul:

Any fear of any kind, from any source, for any purpose, that was put upon me, whether I saw fear, read fear, heard fear, or experienced fear. It has no place in me. I loose it from my soul in Jesus' Name.

I choose with my will to loose from my soul:

Anything that would steal my destiny: any lies, any deceit that was done against me or spoken to me. I will not receive those words in Jesus' Name.

Let's Ponder!

Ask the Holy Spirit to speak and reveal to you other weights or negative attachments that you need to loose from your soul. Then use the loosing sentence stem and speak release from your soul.

Step 2: Binding to Your Soul

To complement the loosing step, you should bind to your soul the good things from the scripture about who God says you are. The sentence stem looks like this:

> I choose with my will, as a believer in Jesus Christ, to bind to my soul. . . [positive truths and attributes].

We invite you to declare these statements as a way to bind the good things of God to your soul:

I choose with my will, as a believer in Jesus Christ, to bind to my soul:

- the love of God
- the life of God
- the joy of the Lord
- His creativity
- His expectation
- His celebration
- His wisdom
- His extreme discernment
- His love for life
- His passion for people, and
- His hope for people.

I bind these things to my soul in Jesus Name.

I choose with my will to bind to my soul, my identity in Christ including: (*relevant identity statements from Appendices A, B, and C*).

In addition, I choose with my will to bind to my soul: (*any or all of the fruit of the Spirit including love, joy, peace, patience, kindness, goodness, faithfulness, gentleness, and self-control*).

Finally, I choose with my will to bind to my soul:

- Witty ideas
- Creativity
- the enjoyment of life itself
- the possibilities of every new day, bringing something new to me.

I bind to my soul love for Jesus Christ, the Father, and Holy Spirit. I choose Their will, Their way.

A Further Note about Binding

An application of using the keys of the kingdom that you may be familiar with is binding the works of the devil in a spiritual warfare context. The phrasing goes something like this:

Satan, I bind you and your work over _____ and I break your strongholds in his or her life, in Jesus Name.

We suggest another potent approach to binding: *commanding* the angelic host of heaven to destroy evil platforms. *You are a commander, so command!* Here are the sentence stems: :

I take authority over all the power of the enemy concerning _____. I invite the host of heaven to be my weapon.

I send the host of heaven to pull down the strongholds of darkness over _____.

I command the host of heaven to shred, dislodge, dismantle, and destroy every evil platform that has been formed against _____, or by _____.

Host of heaven, destroy every evil platform of: _____.

- pride
- rebellion
- rejection (orphan spirit)
- hopelessness
- selfishness
- unbelief
- spiritual blindness
- deception
- depression
- poverty mentality
- defeat
- fatigue
- fear
- grief, and
- a negative outlook

Declare and speak these statements over your soul periodically when you sense your soul has become a little contaminated and needs a cleansing. Keep your heart clean and pure before the Lord and walk in the Spirit!

Let's Internalize and Apply!

1. What are the two steps of a soul check-up?

   _____

   _____

   _____

2. T/F Doing a soul check-up is a Putting Off and a Putting On. _____

3. What does the step of loosing from your soul release off of you?

   _____

   _____

   _____

4. What does the step of binding to your soul do for you?

   _____

   _____

   _____

5. T/F The words binding and loosing in scripture are legal or governmental terms. _____

Chapter 18

Shortcuts To An Upgrade

And do not be conformed to this world [default to the old man], *but be transformed* [upgraded] *by the renewing of your mind* [to the new man].
(*Romans* 12:2, brackets added)

As we draw our journey of activation to an end, we want to share a final perspective that we learned after our wilderness experience. We are the first to tell you that we have not fully attained this perspective, but we are on our way.

God is really good at accelerating our learning. In fact, He specializes in it. He makes circumstances a shortcut to our learning. A shortcut accelerates you.

But you may push back and say, *"My situation does not feel like God is accelerating me. I don't understand why I have to go through this. And, when will it be over? It's taking so long."* You are asking the WHY and the WHEN questions, when you need to be asking the WHAT question: *Lord, what do you want to be for me now to accelerate the upgrade in my identity?*

Remember, you are on a transitional journey from a sin consciousness view to an upgraded righteousness view of yourself. Activation is the process that develops this upgraded righteousness consciousness view in you. God has placed you on His accelerated plan to move to full personhood in Christ.

As a result of *implanting* the Word in our soul and *implementing* the activation and soul cleansing processes, your soul is becoming more conformed to our God-image – the image of Christ. Your identity in Christ, your view of who and what God is, and the development of the fruit of the Spirit are simultaneously upgraded in you.

Let's now look at one more perspective that will facilitate the activation process.

Shortcuts Are A Gift

All circumstances, difficulties, and obstacles are *shortcuts* to give you an upgrade, to elevate you, to teach you there is a whole new design of you that needs to come out.

The three persons of the Godhead are showing you who you are. They are teaching you to think on a heavenly level rather than on this level down here. Your circumstances are accelerating opportunities to grow-up into Christ in all things. You are learning how to get full and stay full to step into your inheritance. Everything in life is customized to teach you so that you can become like Jesus.

We often don't realize how amazing and brilliant we are in Christ. We don't realize His majesty, His supremacy, that He has conquered everything. He came to bring heaven to earth and teach us to be citizens of heaven here on the earth. *As He is, so are we in this world* (I Jn 4:17). This is what we are learning through the shortcuts that our situations provide.

Your circumstances are not the problem; your perception of your circumstances is the problem.

If you are in Christ, and seated with Him in heaven, so are all of your circumstances! When you put your circumstances into Christ, they have to line up with His purpose.

Take each circumstance and put it into Jesus surrounded by the presence of God. Look at the problem the way He would look at it: as a way to upgrade your identity into a more mature righteousness view of yourself. God goes to great lengths to teach you how to *live* in Him, how to *walk* in Him, and how to *be* in Him.

Let's Ponder!

What is it God wants to be for you now that He couldn't be for you before? God wants to be something different for you in each circumstance.

Never tackle a negativity or problem on the same level as it appears.

A negativity or a problem is shortcut designed to elevate you. How else do you expect to get an upgrade?

What if upgrades come in all kinds of shapes and sizes? What if the Lord has designed a whole series of circumstances to give you an upgrade? What if most of the circumstances are negative? Wouldn't it be just like God to park an upgrade right next to a problem? Suddenly there is a blessing that is available on your worst day.

The challenge: When you live in a world-centered culture, you only see the problem. You may not even think there is something brilliant next to the problem — because you are so used to dealing with the negative. Isn't it just like the goodness of God to put something wonderful next to something awful.

> *"God causes all things to work together for good. . ."* Romans 8:28

Possibilities, Not Problems

All circumstances are designed to teach you about possibilities. There are no problems in heaven, only possibilities.

All things are possible to him who believes. Mark 9:23

> *Jesus said to them, "With people this is impossible, but with God all things are possible.* Matthew 19:26

Notice that the above scripture does **not** say, "With God, all things are *problems*." It says that with God all things are possible. There are only possibilities in heaven.

All things are now possible. So we're going to have to come to terms with favor, goodness, possibilities, power, majesty – everything turning out good all the time! Is what you are believing elevating you or killing you?

Giant killers turn problems into possibilities. They create an atmosphere around themselves of the presence of God to face each new problem.

Seek the presence of God in your circumstances. Where is Jesus standing right now in your circumstance? Go stand right next to Him.

Ask Jesus:

> "*How do You see my circumstance from a heavenly perspective?*"
>
> "*What do You want to do in this situation?*"
>
> "*What do You want to be for me now?*"

As we learned earlier, don't ask the "Why" question. Why me? Why now? Why this? Because the why question seldom gets answered on earth. Holy Spirit is training you to see things as He sees them.

Press in to how He sees your situation! Because if you don't accept the heavenly version of your circumstance, you'll have to accept the world's version of it (through the lens of the old man) – which is the way the enemy wants you to think about it. You don't want to be led by those circumstances; you want to be led of the Spirit and first upgrade your identity. Then take that upgraded identity into your circumstance.

Holy Spirit takes everything from Jesus and discloses it to you. The role of the Holy Spirit is to tell you what Jesus is doing, what God is for you now. It's relational. You are learning how to be upgraded in the image of God.

Sometimes when you encounter an obstacle and there is no way through it, God doesn't want you to push through it; He wants to elevate you to a higher level.

When you get an obstacle you can't push through – that's impossible – the Lord is saying:

"*You are done on this level. I put this thing there because I don't want you walking on this level anymore. I want you to walk on a higher level.*"

You have to beat the devil on the level you are on and receive the upgrade in your identity. With each upgrade comes a new anointing and giftings for the next level. So when God determines you are done on a level, He will put an obstacle in front of you that you can't get through. God is saying,

"I don't want you getting through the obstacle, I put it there to elevate you to a different level. You are finished on this level. I need you to come up higher."

Let's Ponder!

Each circumstance/situation is an opportunity for the Lord to upgrade your identity in Him – who you are in Him. Do you have unclaimed upgrades available to you in Christ?

Let's Internalize and Apply!

1. All circumstances, difficulties, and obstacles are shortcuts to give you an upgrade. What does this mean?

   _____

   _____

   _____

2. If you are in Christ, and seated with Him in heaven, then what else is also in heaven?

   _____

   _____

   _____

3. T/F A negativity or a problem is a shortcut designed to downgrade you. _____

4. All circumstances are designed to teach you about _____?

5. T/F With God, all things are problems. _____

6. Giant killers turn problems into _____?

7. T/F When God determines you are done on a level, He will put an obstacle in front of you that you can't get through. _____

Chapter 19

An Upgrade of a Different Sort

In our journey, we have been learning about our identity in Christ and the Activation and recircuiting processes that upgrade that identity. We have learned to remove negative attachments from our soul. Now we will discover the Holy Spirit's most powerful way of upgrading us.

There are three prepositions used in Scripture associated with the ministry of the Holy Spirit. The three prepositions are *with*, *in*, and *upon* the believer. Holy Spirit is *with* us to convince us that we need a Savior. When we receive Christ, we receive a measure of the Holy Spirit *in* us (we are the temple of the Spirit).

The believer receives the Holy Spirit *upon* when Jesus baptizes us in the Holy Spirit to receive the *person* and *power* of Holy Spirit. This is empowerment for ministry.

> *Then there appeared to them divided tongues, as of fire, and one sat **upon** each of them. And they were all filled with the Holy Spirit and began to speak with other tongues, as the Spirit gave them utterance.* Acts 2:3-4 NKJV

> *But you will receive power when the Holy Spirit has come **upon** you; and you shall be My witnesses both in Jerusalem, and in all Judea and Samaria, and even to the remotest part of the earth.* Acts 1:8

Holy Spirit is the Person with the power Who upgrades us in major ways!

Here is the big picture:

> The Father gave us His very best gift: His only Begotten Son.
> Jesus gave us His best gift: the gift of the Holy Spirit.
> Holy Spirit gave us His best gift: the gift of tongues.

Receiving the Holy Spirit *upon* is referred to as receiving the baptism in the Holy Spirit. The outward evidence of the Spirit upon you is the anointing to speak in a heavenly language that is not your native language.

The language you receive when you speak in tongues is customized to you. Holy Spirit knows all the languages in heaven and on earth. I Cor. 13:1 *"if I speak with the tongues* [glossa] *of men and of angels."* Holy Spirit has a much bigger search engine than Google and gives the very best language to you. *Glossa* means a language, and it is the root word for the English word glossary – the words that comprise a language. Keep in mind that we are learning about another way that God upgrades us.

When you pray in tongues, you are agreeing with your destiny book in heaven. Before you were born, the Father wrote out an entire volume – a destiny book — of the good things that He planned for you to accomplish in your life.

And in Your book were all written the days that were ordained for me, when as yet there was not one of them. Psalm 139:16

So when you pray in tongues (your spirit language), you speak in alignment with your destiny book in heaven. You are agreeing with heaven, and the assignments the Lord gives you that align with your destiny, your purpose, and calling.

In order to fulfill that destiny, the Holy Spirit desires to upgrade your born-again spirit with the spiritual resources you need to fulfill the next step of your destiny, purpose, and calling.

An Upgrade of a Different Sort

Uploading and Downloading

Let us share a metaphor with you that we think will help.

Most of us have had experience uploading a file from our computer to someone else on the Internet as well as downloading information over the Internet to our computer.

- To upload, you might attach a file to an email and send it to a business – an insurance company, loan company, or some other business – or to a friend.

- To download, you might request a document be downloaded to, say, DropBox, from a company's website or a ministry's website.

Speaking in tongues can be likened to the uploading and downloading process[9]. God established speaking in tongues as a special way to transfer His power and spiritual resources into you to upgrade you for the next season of your calling.

Take a look at this illustration:

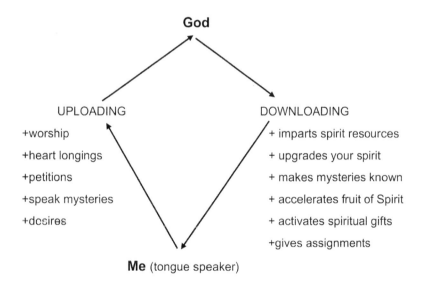

Uploading and Downloading]

---

[9] Lon Stettler, *Activating the Present-Day Ministry of the Holy Spirit* (Xulon Press, 2021), 97-98

Uploading: When you pray in your spirit language, you "upload" your worship, heart longings, petitions (requests), and you speak mysteries directly to God.

Downloading: As you continue to pray in tongues, you "download" resources into your spirit which you need in order to fulfill your assignments from God. God is downloading from His Spirit hard drive to your spirit hard drive when you need it. To be upgraded in your spirit, you must "pray through" until you sense that you have received the download.

Each Download = An Upgrade

As we have learned, the Activation process begins with hearing the Word. Each word (rhema word, prophetic word, dream, and vision) you receive from God has an assignment upon it. Recall that Isaiah 55:11 MSG stated: "*So will the words that come out of my mouth... do the work I sent them to do, they'll complete the assignment I gave them.*" The word with an assignment upon it at some point will meet its moment – the activation.

In order for you to complete each assignment the Lord give you, the Holy Spirit desires to download the anointings, calling, and mantles which upgrade you with the grace and spiritual resources you need to accomplish it. Each download that you receive gives you an upgrade. You will need to receive one or more downloads – or upgrades – to fulfill the assignment He has entrusted to you.

> Each download that you receive gives you an upgrade.

In summary, receiving one or more downloads from Holy Spirit as you pray in your heavenly language is a very powerful way of receiving His supernatural upgrades. Your identity is continually upgraded to empower you to fulfill your destiny and purpose – your calling.

Example: An Upgrade of a Different Sort

The fourth chapter of Acts is a clear example of this upgrading process in action. Peter and John were preaching the gospel of the Kingdom and the power of the resurrected Christ to save and heal. The rulers, elders, and high priests commanded Peter and John not to speak or teach about the name of Jesus. When they were threatened further, Peter and John returned and reported what had happened to the other apostles and disciples.

This assembled group began to pray, connecting what was occurring to the purposes of God in scripture. They asked the Lord for three things: boldness to speak God's word, that God would extend His hand to continue healing, and that signs and wonders would be done through the name of Jesus. Acts 4:31 says:

> *And when they had prayed, the place where they had gathered together was shaken, and they were all filled with the Holy Spirit and began to speak the word of God with boldness.*

All members of the assembled group were filled with the Holy Spirit (as on the Day of Pentecost) and received a new download of spiritual resources and power. They were upgraded with what was needed for the next season and assignment before them.

Notice they did not ask the WHY ("Why is this persecution happening to us?") or the WHEN ("When will this be over?") questions, but they focused on the WHAT ("Lord, do whatever Your hand and Your purpose has destined to occur") and the HOW ("Lord, would you grant that we are empowered to speak your word with confidence?") questions. As a result, the download upgraded them for what was next.

Without the Holy Spirit, we can do nothing. With the person and power of Holy Spirit, we can live the Spirit-filled life and be His upgraded powerful sons and daughters in the earth.

(To learn more about the ministry of the Holy Spirit, we recommend that you read the book, *Activating the Present-Day Ministry of the Holy Spirit,* written by Lon Stettler. Available at Amazon, Barnes & Noble, and Xulon Press.)

Let's Ponder!

Ask Jesus to baptize you in the Holy Spirit and you will receive a heavenly language that will upgrade you for your assignments from Him.

Let's Internalize and Apply!

1. What does it mean when a believer receives the Holy Spirit upon him or her?

   _____

   _____

   _____

2. The Holy Spirit gave us His best gift. What is that gift?

   _____

   _____

   _____

3. In the analogy of Uploading and Downloading when speaking in your heavenly language, when does the upgrade occur?

   _____

   _____

   _____

4. T/F Each download that you receive gives you an upgrade. _____

Section 6:

Activating Prayers
Developing Your 'Righteousness Conscious'

Growing into Full Personhood

Your soul is catching up with what has transpired in your born-again spirit as you move toward full personhood (a "mature man" in Eph. 4:13) – from glory to glory. Your mind and heart are being "transformed by the renewing your mind" (Rom. 12:2), and you are conformed to your God-image – the image of Christ. The end goal of the Activation process is to move you from a 'sin-consciousness' to developing the gold standard of a 'righteousness consciousness.'

The truth of each statement in the following chapters is organized into daily devotions so that you can systematically activate each truth about your born-again spirit. Each day, review the previous day's statements before moving on to the next statement. Follow the four steps of the Activation process to apply each statement.

1. **Hear the Word.** Look up and read out loud the Scriptures associated with each statement and meditate on them in your quiet time. Ask the Holy Spirit to illuminate each Scripture and truth and give you fresh insight of that truth. Hear His voice and in your heart begin to see this truth about you in your mind's eye. View each statement as how God the Father sees you in your born-again spirit, the real 'you.'

2. **Believe the Word.** Begin to believe and accept each statement and accompanying Scriptures. Make the truth of that statement your own – begin to own that statement about you. Really own it. Embrace it with your mind, your heart, and your feelings.

3. **Speak the Word.** Now confess the new statement and truth about you. You activate what you believe when you speak out every good thing in your born-again spirit.

4. **Take Corresponding Action (Do the Word).** Finally, begin to live out the truth that you are believing and saying. Really own the new truth. Put this new truth into positive action. You will know that you fully embrace it when the new truth becomes the "new you."

Activation becomes complete when your soul — mind, will, and emotions – are in 100% agreement and alignment with what has transpired in your born-again spirit. Activation shows up in how you *think*, *feel* and *talk* about yourself, and in your *habits*. You can picture the reality of that truth about you in your mind's eye. You develop an 'emotional resilience' in your new identity. Others see it in your *attitudes* and *actions*. You are one step closer to developing a righteousness conscious. One step closer to being conformed to the image of Christ.

This section contains a chapter devoted to each of the three 'I Am' profiles introduced at the beginning of this book regarding "who you are" in your born-again spirit.

- 'I am Accepted' Profile
- 'I am Secure' Profile
- 'I am Significant' Profile

Chapter 20

Activating Your 'I Am Accepted' Profile

We each have a need to belong and feel accepted. This is true in our relationships with people but especially true in our relationship with our Heavenly Father.

The statements in this chapter focus on the portion of your born-again spirit which relate to God's acceptance of you.

<u>*I Have Acceptance*</u>

<u>*Day 1*</u>

I am *totally accepted* by and *well pleasing* to God.
Read aloud Romans 15:7; Ephesians 1:6; Matthew 3:17; Mark 1:11

Your acceptance is found at the Cross because the Father was fully satisfied with Jesus's payment for your sins. Now, your heavenly Father assesses you based on what Jesus has done.
To the <u>extent</u> that God the Father is *satisfied* with Jesus' finished work, He is *satisfied with you!*

Question: *Is God satisfied with you?*

Answer: This is the wrong question. The real question should be: Is the Father satisfied with the cross of Jesus?

Ephesians 1:6 NKJV says you are "accepted in the Beloved", and Romans 15:7 states "accept one another, just as Christ also accepted us to the glory of God."

The original question (*Is God satisfied with you?*) puts the attention on *My Doing* when the real issue is *His Doing* based on His finished work. Our adversary deceptively keeps trying to move our attention to the *My Doing* column rather than staying focused on the His *Doing column*, putting the attention on self rather than Jesus. We must keep the focus on the right side of the chart, *His Doing*.

Another Question: *Is God pleased with you?*

Notice, once again, the question is pulling you to the *My Doing* side of the chart, and away from the finished work of Christ, *His Doing*.

The real question is: *Is God pleased with Jesus?* In Matthew 3:17, the Father said, "this is My beloved Son, in whom I am well pleased." To the extent that the Father is pleased with Jesus' finished work, He is pleased with you!

Activation prayer:

I believe and declare that, in my born-again spirit, I am totally accepted by my Heavenly Father because Jesus was totally accepted by His Father. My acceptance is complete and permanent. Furthermore, I believe and declare that I am well pleasing to my Heavenly Father because Jesus was well pleasing to His Father. The Father was very satisfied with His work on the Cross. I choose to embrace the fact that I am totally accepted and fully pleasing to my Heavenly Father. I now see myself as totally accepted and fully pleasing to God.

Day 2

I am *righteous* and holy (without blame before Him).
Read aloud Eph. 4:22-24; II Cor. 5:21; I Cor. 3:17; I Pet. 2:5, 9

Let's unpack Ephesians 4:22 – 24: . . .*lay aside the old man* [kind, or race] *and be renewed* [come up to a higher level] *in the spirit of your mind, and put on the new* [not existed before] *self* [new kind or race of man] *which in the likeness of God has been created* [made out of nothing physical] *in righteousness and holiness*. . .

You are now a member of a new race of people – the *saints* race, or the church race. You are part of a people who never existed before – a new kind of man now seated at the right hand of the Father.

As a member of the saints race of people, you are superior to the first man, Adam. While Adam was created in innocence, you have been created in righteousness! And while Adam had authority and dominion over the earth, you have authority in *both* heaven and earth.

Our mortal bodies are here on earth, but our born-again spirits are seated with Christ Jesus at the right hand of the Father. It is a *mystery* and a *paradox* that we can be functioning in our natural bodies here on earth while at the same time our spirits are seated and functioning from the right hand of God in heavenly places in Christ! Your born-again spirit, this treasure in an earthen vessel, is a force to be reckoned with in both heaven and earth!

You are *righteous* and *holy* in your born-again spirit based on the finished work of Christ. The key to remember is you are righteous and holy in your *being* (born-again spirit) before you become so in your *doing* (actions). Make sure you don't confuse your *being* with your *doing*.

Righteous means you have right standing with the Father with all the rights, privileges, and benefits of a son. And *holy* means you are pure like God, without sin.

Activation prayer:

I believe and declare that I am both righteous and holy in my born-again spirit based on the complete work of Christ on the Cross. To the extent that Jesus was righteous and holy in the eyes of His Father, so I am righteous and holy to God. I reject any image in my mind that shows me to be inferior or unworthy in God's sight. I embrace and see myself as holy and righteous in my spirit. Righteous and holy is who I am regardless of the mistakes I've made, or the labels others have tried to put on me, the lies of the enemy, or my own negative self-talk. Because I see myself as righteous and holy, I am now developing a 'righteousness consciousness' of who I am on the inside.

<u>Day 3</u>

I am *perfect, complete, and mature*.
Read aloud Hebrews 10:14; 12:23

At this very moment, your born-again spirit is as perfect and complete as it'll ever be throughout all eternity. You are perfect and complete in your born-again spirit! Your born-again spirit is—right now—as *perfect*, *mature*, and *complete* as Jesus Himself.

Activation prayer:

I believe and declare that I am perfect, complete, and mature in my born-again spirit. I am as perfect, complete, and mature as Jesus is. As Jesus is NOW, so am I in this world! My born-again spirit is as perfect, complete, and mature right now as it will ever be throughout eternity.

Day 4

I am *reconciled* to God and *adopted* as His child.
Read aloud Romans 5:11; Ephesians 1:5

As a result of the finished work of Christ, you have a position of being totally reconciled to the Father. Your Heavenly Father totally embraces you, wrapping His loving arms around you. There is nothing that stands between you and the loving Heavenly Father. You are fully reconciled to The Father based on both the *redemptive* work and the *propitiatory* work of Christ on the Cross. The fiery indignation of the Father toward your sin is totally and completely satisfied.

In fact, Jesus made a double payment for all sins for all time, taking the full brunt of the punishment you deserved, satisfying God's justice (Is. 40:2). As a result, God has adopted you as His child because He passionately loves you and totally accepts you. When the Father looks at you, He sees Jesus.

Activation prayer:

I believe and declare that in my born-again spirit I am totally reconciled to the Father because Jesus has overwhelming paid for my sins and has removed all barriers between me and my Heavenly Father. I declare that I am adopted as a child of the Most High God. Even when I sin, it does not separate me in my relationship with the Father because I am a reconciled, adopted child of God who occasionally sins. When the Father looks at me, He sees Jesus!

Day 5

I am *approved* and *fully qualified* to share in the fullness of His inheritance.
Read aloud 1 Thessalonians 2:4; Colossians 1:12

God has *fully approved* you because He fully approved the finished work of Jesus. To the extent that Jesus was approved, you are approved!

Coupled with that approval, God has *completely qualified* you in your standing before Him! He has qualified you with all His blessings through the shed blood of Jesus Christ on the cross, and His burial and resurrection. He has given you the gift of no-condemnation.

All your *disqualifications* exist in the *natural* realm. You live and operate in the *supernatural* (spiritual) realm where God has *qualified* you with His favor. God has fully qualified you in your born-again spirit.

The enemy tries to pour accusations on you using the *voice of a legalist* to <u>disqualify</u> you. The enemy uses the law and commandments to show your failures, to put a *spotlight on how your behavior has disqualified you* from fellowship with God, pointing out how undeserving you are of His acceptance, love, and blessings. *Put the spotlight on the finished work of Christ*, who on the cross took your condemnation and qualified you to receive God's acceptance, love, and favor forever!

Activation prayer:

I believe and declare that in my born-again spirit I am fully approved by God based on the finished work of Christ. As a result, I am now fully qualified in my standing before God to experience all of His spiritual blessings in heavenly places in Christ. I live and operate in the spiritual realm where God has qualified me with His favor. I reject all of the accusations of the enemy to disqualify me. Those accusations are an assault against my sonship (personhood) in Christ and therefore I reject them. I see myself now as fully approved and qualified by God and the enemy cannot take it from me. My approval and qualification through Christ cannot be taken from me, revoked, or reversed. God has fully approved and qualified me in my born-again spirit.

<u>Day 6</u>

I am *chosen* by God, holy and dearly loved.
Read aloud Colossians 3:12; Ephesians 1:4; I Peter 2:9; Jeremiah 1:5

You did not choose God but He chose you before the foundation of the world. He chose you in Christ to be holy and deeply loved. You are part of the chosen race, a person of God's own possession. You have always been on God's mind. In your born-again spirit, see yourself as He sees you as one *chosen* to be loved.

Activation prayer:

I believe and declare that I am chosen of God before the foundation of the world. Before I was formed in my mother' womb, God knew me. And before I was born, God set me apart for His purpose and appointed me to fulfill a specific destiny that He custom designed. I reject every notion that says God does not have a good plan for my life. I have always been on God's mind. In my born-again spirit, I see myself as He sees me: as one chosen to be loved. I am deeply loved, highly valued, and highly favored.

Day 7

**I am a *new creation* in Christ, a *saint* (a "holy one"),
and a member of a *chosen race*, a *royal priesthood*, a *holy nation*.**
Read aloud 2 Corinthians 5:17-18; Galatians 6:15; Romans 1:7; Colossians 1:2;
I Peter 2:9-10; 2 Peter 1:4

In your born-again spirit, you are a *new creation*, a new *chosen race* of people that has never existed before. You are a new "kind" of people. Your born-again spirit has taken on the divine nature of Christ. You are a saint (a "holy one"), the term used most often to refer to Christians. You are royalty in this new race that is holy and righteous, and a person God now possesses and lives within. You are no longer a sinner, but a saint – a saint who occasionally sins.

Activation prayer:

I believe and declare that I am a new creation, a chosen member of a new race of people. I declare that I am a saint, a holy one, in whom God has taken up residence. As a new creation, I no longer see myself as a sinner but a <u>saint</u>. I remove the image of a 'sin-consciousness' from my mind and replace it with the image of having a 'righteousness-consciousness." I now have the divine nature of Jesus Christ on the inside of me.

Day 8

**I am a *masterpiece*, who is *fearfully* and *wonderfully made*
and *crowned* with *glory* and *honor*.**
Read aloud Psalms 139:14, Ephesians 2:10; Hebrews 2:7

Because you are a new creation and a partaker of His divine nature, you are a masterpiece to God! You are a work of art – one of a kind.

You are fearfully [to stand in awe of] and wonderfully made. Not only that, God has crowned you with His glory and honor. So you are *completely amazing* and *awesome* and more *wonderful* that you know.

Picture it: The Creator of the universe, who created you, takes one step back and looks at you and says, "you're awesome." He stands in awe of you, His creation.

When God looks at Himself in a mirror, He sees *you*; He sees God in the mirror!

God *created* you, and now *recreated* you (you are now a 'new creation'), in such a way that we provide an accurate reflection of His glory back to Him and onto the world.

Activation prayer:

I believe and declare that I am a masterpiece to God. I am awesome and wonderfully made by God, and He put the finishing touch on me by crowning me with His glory and honor. He looks at me every day and says, "You are awesome!" I choose to see myself as my Father sees me — a highly-valued masterpiece, one of a kind!

Day 9

I am a *child* of the Most High God!
Read aloud John 1:12; Romans 8:16; Galatians 3:26; 4:6

As a new creation in Christ, who is fearfully and wonderfully made *and* crowned with glory and honor, you are a *child* of the Most High God! What a privilege! As a child or son of God, you have been given *authority* as a believer in Christ Jesus. As a child of God, God has sent the Spirit of His Son into our hearts, crying "Abba! Father!" Because you, as a child of God, are now co-seated with Christ at the right hand of the Father, you now have authority in both heaven and earth.

Activation prayer:

I believe and declare that in my born-again spirit, I am a child of the Most High God. God has sent the Spirit of His Son into my spirit and now I am His child. As a child of God, I now have the right to exercise authority in both heaven and earth. What a privilege I have! I now see myself as His child, and He is my loving Father, and I have authority to exercise dominion in my world!

Day 10

I am *completely forgiven* of all of my sins – past, present, and future.
Read aloud I John 2:1-2; Hebrews 9:12, 15; 10:10, 14

The completeness of forgiveness is covered in Chapter 4: The War is Over and God is Not Mad.

Activation prayer:

I believe and declare that in my born-again spirit, I am completely forgiven of all my sins – past, present, and future. Based on the finished work of Christ, God has imputed (credited) righteousness to me and has not imputed sin. God's forgiveness of my sins is not on a timeline because God does not forgive in installments. Two thousand years ago, Jesus paid for all my sins – once for all time. This is such a freeing way to live!

Day 11

I am *free from condemnation* because Jesus has given me the gift of no-condemnation, and I am now a *joint heir* with Christ, sharing His inheritance with Him.
Read aloud Romans 8:1, 17, 34

You now have been given the gift of no-condemnation in your born-again spirit and have been made a joint heir with Christ.

The feeling of condemnation is an <u>assault</u> against your sonship in Christ. That assault is either from Satan or your conscience, but it is not from God. Because you are righteous, holy, and free from condemnation in your born-again spirit, you must push back against the charge of condemnation from the enemy. Do not accept the charge of the enemy. You are now a joint heir with Christ and you share in His inheritance, so reject any condemning assault against your sonship. (See Chapter 11).

Activation prayer:

I believe and declare that in my born-again spirit I am free from all condemnation against me. Jesus took the full brunt of the punishment for my sins so that I can live free of condemnation. I keep my eyes on Jesus' finished work for me, and not my own works. I will not accept any accusation or condemnation for sin that Jesus already paid for nearly two-thousand years ago. I choose to fully accept the gift of no-condemnation and live as a joint heir with Christ and share in His full inheritance!

Day 12

I am *deeply and tenderly loved* by God, and He calls me a *friend* of God.
Read aloud John 15:14-15; John 3:16; Jeremiah 31:3

You are a *friend* of God and are deeply and tenderly loved by God. God loves you with an everlasting love, and this love sent Jesus to die on the Cross for you. God calls you His friend, and Jesus will make known to you all things that He has heard from His Father.

Activation prayer:

I believe and declare that I am deeply loved by God in my born-again spirit and He calls me His friend. I walk in and bask in God's everlasting love for me. As I am God's friend, Jesus (through the Holy Spirit) makes known to me all that the Father has shared with the Son that pertains to me. Thank you Jesus that you view me as Your friend. I likewise see Jesus as my personal Friend!

Day 13

I am *highly favored* and *crowned with favor*.
Read aloud Ephesians 1:6; Luke 1:28; Proverbs 4:9

God the Father has made you a "highly favored" (Greek: *charitoo*) one in His sight. Ephesians 1:6 NKJV says, "*to the praise of the glory of His grace* [unmerited favor], *by which He made us accepted* [highly favored] *in the Beloved*. God is saying to you, "Greetings, highly favored one, I the Lord am with you!" In fact, He has honored you by crowning you with His favor.

Just as Noah (Gen. 6:8), David (Acts 7:46), and Joseph (Gen. 39:4) found favor in the sight of God, you have also found favor with God! God has declared that you are His "highly favored one!"

Activation prayer

I believe and declare that in my born-again spirit, I am a highly favored one. You have crowned me with your favor. Now, I live and walk in God's favor, because His favor is for a lifetime (Psalms 30:5). I declare that the favor of God surrounds me as with a shield (Psalms 5:12). I simply believe that I am highly favored! I now stand on <u>favor</u> ground, and no longer do I stand on 'condemnation ground'! I now see myself with a favor-consciousness – that inner knowing that I am highly favored! I will not let anyone take my crown of favor.

Day 14

I am *greatly blessed* because I have God's spoken blessing on my head, and therefore I cannot be cursed.
Read aloud Genesis 1:28; Ephesians 1:3; Numbers 23:8, 20; Proverbs 10:6

Before anyone attempted to put a curse (or a negative label) on you, God put His commanded blessing upon you that cannot be reversed. God has commanded a blessing upon you, and when He blesses, then it cannot be revoked (Numbers 23:20). Now God has blessed you with every spiritual blessing found in heavenly places in Christ. God has qualified you to share in the inheritance of the saints! Proverbs 10:6 declares that the blessings of God are on your head.

Activation prayer:

I believe and declare that God has spoken His commanded blessing upon me from the very beginning and that the blessing cannot be reversed. I declare that in my born-again spirit I possess God's commanded blessing and every spiritual blessing in heavenly places in Christ Jesus. I now receive the blessing of God and nothing and no one in the devil's kingdom – including the devil himself – can stop it. God has blessed me and the enemy cannot reverse it. Therefore, I reject and do not accept any curse or negative label that anyone would attempt to put on me. I now see myself as one whom God has permanently blessed and His spoken blessing is on my head!

Day 15

I am *redeemed* from the curse of the law, *purchased* by God.
Read aloud Galatians 3:13; I Peter 1:18-19; Acts 20:28; I Corinthians 6:19-20: Deuteronomy 28:8

Jesus purchased your redemption from the curse of the law, as He paid for all your sins. Based on Jesus' redemptive work on the Cross, you are brought back in full relationship to the Father. (Refer to the *Salvation Triangle* in Chapter 10). You were redeemed by the precious blood of Christ. You are no longer cursed but *blessed*. Before anyone tries to put a spoken curse on you, remember that God has put His commanded blessing on you! And that commanded blessing cannot be reversed or revoked.

Activation prayer:

I believe and declare that I am completely redeemed from the curse of the law because Jesus paid for that penalty on the Cross. I am now redeemed by the blood of Christ. God's commanded blessing on me is permanent, and cannot be reversed or revoked. I see my born-again spirit as completely redeemed and God's commanded blessing is on me forever.

Day 16

I am sanctified **(positionally) as holy to God.**
Read aloud Hebrews 2:11, 10:10; I Corinthians 6:11; I John 5:18

You were sanctified (set-apart) *positionally* (in your born-again spirit) when you accepted Christ as Savior which placed you into the body of Christ. The Holy Spirit is the baptizer and the element we are baptized into is the body of Christ. This occurred at conversion.

Now that you are positionally sanctified because you are born of God, your born-again spirit is holy and cannot (and does not) sin. You are now born of God and the evil one does not touch you!

[Note: The sanctifying work of the Holy Spirit is also a *process (Hebrews 2:11; 10:14; I Peter 1:2)*, which is on-going from the time of conversion until you go to be with the Lord. This is the work

of the Holy Spirit to conform our life to the image of Jesus Christ (Romans 8:29). The Activation process, the subject of this book, is a large part of that sanctifying process.]

Activation prayer:

I believe and declare that I am positionally sanctified and set part to God in my born-again spirit. I am now set apart as holy to God. My born-again spirit is conformed to the image of Christ and being applied in my mind and my heart. In my mind's eye, I now see myself as holy and set-apart not only in my spirit, but also in my soul and my body as well. As one who is born-again and sanctified unto God, I believe and declare that "I am born of God and the evil one does not touch me!"

Chapter 21

Activating Your "I am Secure" Profile

We each have a need to receive and embrace our security in Christ. Our Heavenly Father has you securely in His hand. You belong to Him and He is strong to protect and shield you. He wants you to know that you are secure in your relationship with Him.

The statements in this chapter focus on the portion of your born-again spirit which relate to your security in God.

To activate the truth in each statement, select a daily devotion to focus on each day and follow the four action steps described at the beginning of Section 3.

My Life has Security

Day 17

I am *hidden with Christ* in God.
Read aloud Colossians 3:3; John 10:28-29

Your life is hidden with Christ in God which means you have two layers of protection. First, picture one set of hands around you – the protective hands of the Lord Jesus Christ. Outside of those hands, there are the protective hands of your heavenly Father. Picture both sets of hands hiding you, concealing you, and protecting you. Your hiding place and protection is found in both Jesus and your heavenly Father.

You are so protected that Jesus said that when He gave you eternal life (a born-again spirit), that no one can snatch you out of His hand. He further said no one is able to snatch you out of the Father's hand either. You are safely placed and hidden in Christ . . .in God.

Activation prayer;

I believe and declare that, in my born-again spirit, my life is safely hid in Christ. I picture two sets of protective hands around and about me: the protective hands of the Lord Jesus Christ and the protective, concealing hands of the Father. Because my born-again spirit is safely hidden in Christ and in God, there is no person or devil that can snatch me out of the hands of Jesus Christ or the Father. I am well hidden and protected in God!

Day 18

I am *born again* and the evil one cannot touch me.
Read aloud I John 5:18

What an assurance of your security in Christ! Because you are born-again, you are now a force to be reckoned with! Your born-again spirit is holy and cannot sin. Because you are now born of God, the evil one cannot touch your born-again spirit.

Activation prayer:

I believe and declare that I have a born-again spirit that is holy and without sin. My born-again spirit places and positions me in a secure place in Christ. From that secure position of being seated with Christ in heavenly places I declare that because I am born again, the evil one cannot touch me or anything that is mine. My born-again spirit and my life are divinely protected from the evil one. I believe, declare and activate that the evil one cannot touch me! I have divine protection from the evil one. I put on the whole armor of God that I may be able to further protect my entire life. (Ephesians 6:13-17).

Day 19

I am a *temple* in which God dwells, a *living stone*, being built up in Christ as a spiritual house.
Read aloud I Corinthians 3:16-17; I Peter 2:5

Your born-again spirit is the dwelling place of the Spirit. The Lord has declared that you are a holy temple, a spiritual house. You body is a temple where Christ Jesus lives and has permanence. This should give you a sense of divine security. As this truth is being activated in your soul, He is building a spiritual house with living stones upon the foundation of your temple.

Activation prayer:

I believe and declare that my born-again spirit is not a temporary tabernacle, but a permanent temple in which God dwells. The spiritual house within me is a holy dwelling place full of the life of God.

Day 20

I am *united* to the Lord, one spirit with Him.
Read aloud I Cor. 6:17; Romans 6:5

You are tightly united to the Lord and one spirit with Him in your born-again spirit. Know that in your born-again spirit you are dead to sin, but alive to God in Christ Jesus.

You have the responsibility to safeguard your body from sin and keep it from being used as an instrument of unrighteousness. Failing to do so would be to *violate the unity* you have with the Lord and your spiritual oneness with Him. Sinning *violates the unity* you have with the Lord and your spiritual oneness with Him.

Sinning against your own body involves sinning against the One with whom you are united, allowing sin to reign in your mortal body.

Activation prayer:

I believe and declare that I am tightly united to the Lord and one spirit with Him in my born-again spirit. I declare that in my spirit I am dead to sin but very alive to God because of the unity and oneness I have in Him. I declare that I will guard my life so that I do not violate the unity and spiritual oneness I have with the Lord. I will cherish that unity I have with my Lord Jesus and do not want to violate it in any way.

Day 21

I am *firmly rooted* and built up in Christ.
Read aloud Colossians 2:7

You have already been firmly rooted in Christ Jesus. Being firmly rooted and established in Christ in your born-again spirit is a finished work. It is a done deal. You are secure in Christ because you are deeply and firmly rooted, and His root in you is not shallow. Christ is firmly rooted in your spirit.

Now, the purpose of your Christian journey is allowing Jesus Christ to build you up in Him in the way He chooses. He is the Potter and you are the clay. Allow the Holy Spirit to form you and shape you in the way He chooses to build your inner character to conform to the image of Christ. Be diligent to activate all of the truths about your born-again spirit.

Activation prayer:

I believe and declare that Jesus Christ has been firmly established in me in my born-again spirit. I see myself now as very secure in Christ knowing that He will not leave me or forsake me. Because He is deeply rooted in me, and I am deeply rooted in Him, no one is able to snatch me out of the hands of Jesus Christ. Nor is anyone able to snatch me out of the hands of my heavenly Father. I am daily being established in my faith in Him with a heart full of gratitude.

Day 22

I am so secure that I *cannot be separated* from the love of God.
Read aloud Romans 8:31-39, especially 35 and 39

It is impossible for you to be separated from the love of God! Nothing and no one can separate you from the love of the Father. God the Father cannot and will not separate you from His love. He did not spare His own Son but delivered Him up on the Cross for you.

Likewise, Jesus justified you when He died and was raised from the dead to the right hand of the Father where He prays for you. So no one and nothing can ever separate you from the Father's love. Because you cannot be separated from the love of the Father, in your born-again spirit you are an *overwhelming conqueror* through Christ who loves you!

Activation prayer:

I believe and declare that I cannot be separated from the love of my Father. Both my heavenly Father and my Lord Jesus have done everything so that I will never be separated from their love for me. In my mind's eye, I see myself as surrounded by the loving hands of Jesus, and His hands surrounded by the hands of my loving Heavenly Father. I declare that no one and nothing can ever separate me from the Father's love!

Day 23

I am *established* and *sealed* by God.
Read aloud 2 Cor. 1:21, 22

Being sealed by God indicates *ownership* of your life and it *preserves* you by sealing in your new nature and sealing out contamination. Your born-again spirit is sealed to keep out the impurities and evil, and seal in the new nature (which is righteous, holy, perfect, complete). Sin, and its effects, cannot enter into your spirit. Your born-again spirit retains its original holiness and purity – and will for eternity! As long as this seal remains unbroken, you are preserved blameless in spirit, soul, and body. That seal firmly establishes you in God. Your relationship and foundation in Him is sure and solid.

Activation prayer:

I believe and declare that I am established and sealed by God in my born-again spirit. I declare that I securely belong to Christ and God's seal upon my spirit insures ("seals in") my new nature that is righteous, holy, perfect, blameless, and complete. I have an unshakable confidence in my security in God. I am locked in with God. Because I am sealed and established, there is no one who can snatch me out of the hands of Jesus and there is no one who can snatch me out of the hands of my loving Heavenly Father.

Day 24

I am fully *assured* that all things are working together for good, and *confident* that the *good work* God has begun in me *will be completed.*
Read aloud Romans 8:28-29; Philippians 1:6; Hebrews 2:11; 10:14; I Peter 1:2

Because of the security that you have in Christ, you have the *assurance* that God is working everything together to conform your soul (inner person) to the image of Jesus Christ. This assurance was placed in your born-again spirit at salvation. As with any other truth about your born-again spirit, you must *believe* that this assurance is present in you. This imparted assurance includes the confidence that the good work that God began in you will be taken to completion. This assurance is in your born-again spirit in seed form and when activated, it becomes fully alive in your mind and heart and yields a confident steadfastness.

God working everything together for us is the sanctifying work of the Holy Spirit which is on-going from the time of conversion until you go to be with the Lord. This is the work of the Holy Spirit to conform our life to the image of Jesus Christ. You can have great assurance that God will bring the conforming work to completion!

Activation prayer:

I believe and declare that I have <u>assurance</u> in my born-again spirit that the Father, Jesus, and the Holy Spirit are working and coordinating all things in my life for good. I declare that I have confidence that the good work that God started in my life will be brought to completion, perfection, and maturity. I believe that the Holy Spirit will shepherd the sanctifying process in my life so that my soul is conformed to the image of Christ. I will wholeheartedly embrace that sanctifying process with my mind, will, and emotions.

<u>Day 25</u>

I am *raised* and *seated with Christ* in the heavenly realm and am a *citizen of heaven*
Read aloud Ephesians 2:6,19; Philippians 3:20

Your mortal body is here on earth, but your born-again spirit is seated with Christ Jesus at the right hand of God. It is a *mystery* and *paradox* that you can be functioning in your natural body here on earth while at the same time your spirit is seated and functioning from the right hand of God in heavenly places in Christ. As a result, you are a citizen, not of earth, but of heaven.

Just as Jesus was crucified, buried, resurrected, ascended, and seated at the right hand of His Father, you, too, are co-crucified, co-buried, co-resurrected, co-ascended, and co-seated with Jesus Christ at the right hand of the Father! This is the basis of your authority.

Activation prayer:

"I believe and declare that I am co-crucified, co-buried, co-resurrected, co-ascended, and co-seated with Jesus Christ at the right hand of the Father. This is my spiritual position in the heavenly places in Christ at the right hand of God. This is my spiritual sphere of operation, my warrior headquarters, and command center. I am now, in my born-again spirit, a citizen of heaven. In my mind's eye, I see my spiritual position as 'far above all rule and authority and power and dominion'. As Jesus is <u>now</u>, so am I in this world" (I John 4:17).

Day 26

I am an *overcomer* who is the *head* and not the tail, *above only* and not beneath.
Read aloud I John 4:4; 5:4-5; Deuteronomy 28:13

You are an overcomer in your born-again spirit because greater is He who is in you than he who is in the world! Because you are born of God, you have the power to overcome the world. The key is to believe that, in the core of your spirit man, you are an overcomer. As an overcomer, see yourself as the head in every situation, and not the tail; see yourself as above only and not beneath. See yourself as God the Father sees you – an overcomer!

In the book of Revelation chapters 2 and 3, there are promised blessings for you if you overcome: Eat of the tree of life in the Paradise of God; eat the hidden manna; receive a white stone with a new name written on it; be given authority over nations; receive a white garment so your name will not be erased from the book of life; He will write His name on you signifying you are His; and you get to sit with the Father on His throne.

Activation prayer:

I believe and declare that in my born-again spirit, I am an overcomer! I believe and declare that greater is God who is in me than the enemy who is in the world. As an overcomer, I see myself as the head of every situation that affects me, and I choose not to see myself as the tail any longer. I see myself as above, having the upper hand, in every situation and not below. I know my heavenly Father sees me as an overcomer and I choose to also see myself that same way.

Day 27

I am *strong in the Lord* and in the strength of His might.
Read aloud Ephesians 6:10; 2:6

You are strong, that is, empowered in your born-again spirit. This means you are a *dynamo* because Jesus has imparted His strength and power into your born-again spirit.

Remember, you are *co-seated* with Christ at the right hand of the Father. You are more than able to be strong in your life. Now, the strength that is in you enables you to exercise and exert dominion over every situation that you encounter. You are now a force to overcome immediate resistance.

Activation prayer:

I believe and declare that, in my born-again spirit, I am strong in the Lord, a <u>dynamo</u> that contains the strength and power that Jesus has imparted into me. Because I am co-seated with Christ at the right hand of the Father, I possess the strength to exert dominion over every situation I encounter. I am now a force to be reckoned with and I overcome any immediate resistance. I am strong in the strength of His might!

Chapter 22

Activating Your "I am Significant" Profile

We each have a need to know that our life has meaning and makes a significant contribution and impact on others. Your Heavenly Father wants you to know that your life has great significance! Your life has a purpose, and many of you will feel like you can change the world.

The statements in this chapter focus on the portion of your born-again spirit which relate to the fact that *your life has great significance*. Your life matters and makes an eternal difference.

To activate the truth in each statement, select a daily devotion to focus on each day and follow the four action steps described at the beginning of Section 3.

<u>*My Life has Great Significance*</u>

<u>Day 28</u>

I am the *salt* and a child of *light* in the world.
Read aloud Matthew 5:13-16; I Thessalonians 5:5

Your born-again spirit is characterized by *salt* and *light*, which impacts both your life and the lives of those around you. Your life has great significance! As salt, you flavor and influence the lives of people you interact with each day. The Spirit of Christ in you influences others in a godly way.

As light, you shine and reflect the light of the Holy Spirit to others. You shine brightly in the darkness. You are a child of light, a child of the day. The light you possess in your born-again spirit has a significant effect on the lives of others. The light in you cannot be hidden. Often,

Christians grossly underestimate the power of the light of their born-again spirit on those around them. So let your light shine brightly out of your spirit to others so God in heaven is glorified.

Activation prayer:

I believe and declare that I will release the salt and light nature of my born-again spirit into my soul and life. I release and draw out the preserving influence of my born-again spirit to positively impact not only my life but the lives of others. I will live my life before others in a way that will influence and positively impact others with the nature of Christ. I will not hide the light within my spirit but I release it to others. I choose to let my light shine brightly out of my spirit to others so God in heaven is glorified!

Day 29

I am a *member* of Christ's body and a *coworker* with Him.
Read aloud I Corinthians 3:9; 12:13, 27; 2 Corinthians 6:1

In your born-again spirit, you have been placed as an individual member of the body of Christ. You are God's fellow worker, to flow and work together with Him.

The Holy Spirit is not only <u>in</u> you but also <u>with</u> you. One of the Greek words for 'with' is the word *meta*. Meta means "after with", which means the Holy Spirit works with and through you after you are born again. (There is a different Greek word for 'with', *para*, when the Holy Spirit is drawing us to Christ for repentance and salvation). As one who is a member of the body of Christ, the Holy Spirit will be *meta* (with) you to minister as God's fellow worker in cooperation with Him and other saints. There is an *after-effect* that you are to release and draw out of your born-again spirit.

Activation prayer:

I believe and declare that as a member of the body of Christ and a coworker with Him, I have been fully resourced to have a positive impact on the lives of others. I now draw out of my born-again spirit and release all spiritual resources to minister to others. As such, I declare that the life in my born-again spirit influences me and makes a significant impact in the lives of others.

<u>Day 30</u>

As a branch (channel) of Christ's vine, I am chosen and appointed to bear the fruit of life.
Read aloud John 15:1, 5, 16; Galatians 5:22-23

Your highest calling is to be conformed to the image of Christ in your soul (heart). Your born-again spirit already possesses the nature and image of Christ. The fruit of the Spirit was imparted into your spirit in *seed* form when you were *born* of the Spirit. The fruit are planted in your spirit as nine different *seeds* that are to be watered and cultivated until they grow to maturity in your heart. They are to infiltrate your nature and personality until they become your new nature and way of life.

You are fully resourced to do what God has called you to do. You don't need to ask God to give you the fruit of the Spirit; rather, you already have them resident in your born-again spirit. You've already got the fruit! You simply need to activate them.

Activation prayer:

I believe and declare that I possess the fruit of the Spirit in my born-again spirit. God has appointed me to be a branch and channel of the Christ-fruits. I choose to activate the fruit of the Spirit to flow from my born-again spirit into my heart and all of my life. By faith, I declare and release the fruit of love, joy, peace, patience, kindness, goodness, faithfulness, gentleness, and self-control to flow through me today as a channel of life!

<u>Day 31</u>

I am an *ambassador* of Christ, a *minister* of reconciliation.
Read aloud 2 Corinthians 5:17–20

When you received Jesus Christ as Savior, you were reconciled to God through the finished work of Christ. He imparted His reconciling nature in your born-again spirit to be an ambassador of reconciliation to others. This includes reconciling the unbeliever to God through Christ as well as reconciling one person to another (and you to another person). In addition, you have the *word* of reconciliation in your born-again spirit which contains the substance you are to speak to others to activate reconciliation.

Activation prayer:

I believe and declare that I have the reconciling nature of Christ in my born-again spirit to be an ambassador of reconciliation to others. I declare that I will be sensitive to the leading of my born-again spirit to make sure that I am in right relationship with others, and if not, I will seek reconciliation with him or her. I further declare that I will follow the leading of the Holy Spirit to minister Christ's reconciling nature through me as His ambassador. I <u>am</u> an ambassador of Christ, a minister of reconciliation!

Day 32

I am *an overwhelming conqueror who triumphs in Christ*.
Read aloud Romans 8:31-39, verse 8:37; Deuteronomy 28:13; 2 Corinthians 2:14

No one and nothing can ever separate you from the Father's love. Because you cannot be separated from the love of the Father, in your born-again spirit you are an *overwhelming conqueror* who God leads into triumph in Christ.

Activation prayer:

I believe and declare that I am an overwhelming conqueror in my born-again spirit. I am secure as a conqueror because I cannot be separated from the love of my Father. Both my heavenly Father and my Lord Jesus have done everything so that I will never be separated from their love for me. I declare that no one and nothing can ever separate me from the Father's love. I declare that as a conqueror, I always walk in triumph! In my mind's eye, I see myself as an overwhelming conqueror, the head and not the tail, above and not beneath!

Day 33

I am *called* of God to fulfill my divine destiny as a *king* and *priest* unto God.
Read aloud 2 Timothy 1:9; Revelation 1:6; 5:10

You have a holy calling to fulfill your divine destiny according to His purpose and grace. In your born-again spirit, you have been fully resourced by God to fulfill all that He has called you to do. In your spirit, you have all the spiritual resources (Ephesians 1:3) to draw upon and release.

As a *king*, you are to exercise dominion in the marketplace, your profession, and at home. As a godly person, you are to impact all aspects of society for Kingdom purposes. God is calling His people to superimpose His Kingdom in the business world, politics, the arts and media, athletics, entertainment, medicine, science, and every other area of life.

As a *priest*, you are to apply the spiritual resources of Christ to the needs of the people. Your priestly ministry will often occur inside the local church.

Activation prayer:

I believe and declare that I have a holy calling and destiny to fulfill. I will activate my divine call by reigning and exercising dominion in my sphere of influence – in the marketplace, my profession, and my home. I am the head and not the tail; I am above and not beneath. I declare that I will fulfill my priestly ministry by using the spiritual resources imparted in my born-again spirit to meet the needs of people who God loves. I will fulfill my divine calling!

Appendix A:

You Are Accepted

We each have from God more than we know. Your Heavenly Father has granted you everything you need pertaining to life and godliness (2 Peter 1:3). You are who God says you are.

The statements below focus on the portion of your born-again spirit which relate to your **acceptance** in Christ. To activate the truth in each statement, follow the four Activation steps.

I am Accepted

- I am righteous (Eph. 4:24; II Cor. 5:21); that is, I am the righteousness of God in Christ Jesus.

- I am holy and without blame before God (Eph. 4:24; I Cor. 3:17; I Pet. 2:5, 9)

- I am perfect, complete, and mature in my born-again spirit (Heb. 10:14; 12:23)

- I am reconciled to God and adopted as His child (Rom. 5:11; Eph. 1:5)

- I am redeemed from the curse of the law, purchased by God (Gal. 3:13; I Pet. 1:18-19; I Cor. 6:19-20; Acts 20:28)

- I am totally accepted by God (Rom. 15:7; Eph. 1:5-6 NKJV)

- I am well pleasing to God because I am in Christ Who was well-pleasing to the Father (Matt. 3:17; Mark 1:11)

- I am approved (I Thess. 2:4)

- I am chosen by God, holy and dearly loved (Col. 3:12; I Pet. 2:9)

- I am a friend of God (John 15:15)

- I am a new creation in Christ and therefore a 3rd heaven creation. (II Cor. 5:17-18; Gal. 6:15)

- I am a partaker of His divine nature (2 Pet. 1:4)

- I am a saint (a "holy one") (Eph. 2:19; Rom. 1:7; Col. 1:2)

- I am a masterpiece (His "workmanship") (Eph. 2:10)

- I am crowned with glory and honor (Heb. 2:7)

- I am a child of the Most High God! (John 1:12; Rom. 8:16)

- I am fully qualified to share in the fullness of His inheritance (Col. 1:12).

- I am completely forgiven of all of my sins – past, present, and future (I John 2:1-2; Heb. 9:12, 15; 10:10, 14)

- I am free from condemnation because Jesus has given me the gift of no-condemnation (Rom. 8:1, 34).

- I am deeply and tenderly loved by God (John 3:16; Jer. 31:3)

- I am highly favored (Eph. 1:6; Luke 1:28) and crowned with favor (Prov. 4:9)

- I am greatly blessed and cannot be cursed (Eph. 1:3; Numb. 23:8, 20)

- I am a joint heir with Christ, sharing His inheritance with Him (Rom. 8:17)

- I am sanctified (positionally) as holy to God (Heb. 2:11)

- I am fearfully and wonderfully made (Psalm 139:14)

- I am a member of a chosen race, a royal priesthood, a holy nation (I Pet. 2:9-10)

- I am justified (declared not guilty) by the Blood of Christ (Rom. 5:9)

- I am a victor, not a victim. I have the victory through the Lord Jesus Christ (I Cor. 15:57)

Appendix B:

You Are Secure

We each have from God more than we know. Your Heavenly Father has granted you everything you need pertaining to life and godliness (2 Peter 1:3). You are who God says you are.

The statements below focus on the portion of your born-again spirit which relate to your **security** in Christ. To activate the truth in each statement, follow the four Activation steps.

I am Secure

- I am hidden with Christ in God (Col. 3:3)

- I am born again and the evil one cannot touch me (I John 5:18).

- I am a temple in which God dwells (I Cor. 3:16)

- I am united to the Lord, one spirit with Him (I Cor. 6:17)

- I am firmly rooted and built up in Christ (Col. 2:7)

- I am a living stone, being built up in Christ as a spiritual house (I Pet. 2:5)

- I cannot be separated from the love of God (Rom. 8:35)

- I am securely established and sealed by God (2 Cor. 1:21, 22)

- I am assured that all things are working together for good (Rom. 8:28)

- I am a citizen of heaven (Phil. 3:20)

- I am confident that the good work God has begun in me will be completed (Phil. 1:6)

- I am the head and not the tail; I am above only and not beneath (Deut. 28:13)

- I am co-crucified (Gal. 2:20), co-buried (Rom. 6:4), co-resurrected (Rom. 6:4), co-ascended (Eph. 2:4-6), and co-seated (Eph. 2:6) with Christ in the heavenly realm and have 3rd heaven authority.

- I am strong in the Lord and in the strength of His might. (Eph. 6:10)

Appendix C:

You Are Significant

We each have from God more than we know. Your Heavenly Father has granted you everything you need pertaining to life and godliness (2 Peter 1:3). You are who God says you are.

The statements below focus on the portion of your born-again spirit which relate to your **significance** in Christ. To activate the truth in each statement, follow the four Activation steps.

I am Significance

- I am salt and light in the world (Matt. 5:13-14)

- I am a child of light (Matt. 5:14: I Thess. 5:5)

- I am a branch of Christ's vine, a channel of His life (John 15:1, 5)

- I am a member of Christ's body (I Cor. 12:27)

- I am God's coworker (2 Cor. 6:1; I Cor. 3:9)

- I am chosen and appointed to bear fruit (John 15:16)

- I am a minister of reconciliation (2 Cor. 5:17 – 20)

- I am an ambassador of Christ (II Cor. 5:20)

- I am more than a conqueror (Rom. 8:37)

- I am called of God to fulfill my divine destiny (2 Tim. 1:9)

- I am a king and priest unto God (Rev. 1:6; 5:10)

- I am transformed from glory to glory into God's glory (2 Cor. 3:18)

Appendix D:

What You Have

We each have from God more than we know. Your Heavenly Father has granted you everything you need pertaining to life and godliness (2 Peter 1:3). You have what God says you have.

The statements below focus on the portion of your born-again spirit which relate to what you **have** in Christ. To activate the truth in each statement, follow the four Activation steps.

- I have the "I AMness of God" in me (Gen. 1:26)

- I have eternal life (John 3:15-16; I John 5:13)

- I have peace with and the peace of God (Rom. 5:1; 15:33)

- I have the fullness of the Godhead (John 1:16; Col. 2:9-10).

- I have my conscience cleansed (from dead works and an evil conscience) by the blood of Christ (Heb. 9:14; 10:22).

- I have the favor of God surrounding me like a shield (Ps. 5:12)

- I have the spoken blessings of God on my head (Prov. 10:6)

- I have the abundance of grace [favor] and the gift of righteousness to reign in life (Rom. 5:17)

- I have a commanded blessing on my life (Gen. 15:6; Gal. 3:29), and therefore His blessings are chasing me down and overtaking me (Deut. 28:2, 8).

- I have the mind of Christ (I Cor. 2:16)

- I have been transferred into the kingdom of Christ (Col. 1:13)

- I have been given great and precious promises from God (2 Pet. 1:14)

- I have direct access to God through the Holy Spirit (Eph. 2:18)

- I have all my needs met by God according to His glorious riches in Christ Jesus (Phil. 4:19)

- I have everlasting life (John 6:47)

- I have abundant life (John 10:10)

- I have overcome the world (I John 5:4)

- I have the Greater One living in me, because greater is He who is in me than he that is in the world (I John 4:4)

- I have 3rd heaven authority as a believer in the Lord Jesus Christ (John 1:12-13)

- I have this treasure (Jesus) in this earthen vessel (my body) (2 Cor. 4:7)

If baptized in the Holy Spirit (Spirit "upon"):
- I have received the power of Holy Spirit (Acts 1:8) when I received the baptism in the Holy Spirit.

- I have an anointing from the Holy One (I John 2:20, 27; 2 Cor. 1:21, 22)

Appendix E:

What You Can Do

We each can do what the Bible says we can do. Your Heavenly Father has given you can-do ability and power to do and obey what He commands us to do.

These statements focus on the portion of your born-again spirit which relate to what you **can do** because Christ lives in you mightily. To activate the truth in each statement, follow the four Activation steps.

- I can do all things through Christ who strengthens me (Phil. 4:13).

- I can condemn any accusing word spoken against me because I am righteous (Is. 54:17; Rom. 8:1).

- I can reign in life by Christ Jesus (Rom. 5:17)

- I can approach God with boldness, freedom, and confidence (Eph. 3:12)

- I always triumph in Christ (2 Cor. 2:14)

- I can hear God's voice (John 10:14)

- I can release the government of God through my declarations using the sword of the Word of God.

- I can release the government of God through my decrees extending a scepter as an heir. (Job 22:28; Prov. 8:15)

If baptized in the Holy Spirit (Spirit "upon"):
- I can do greater works than Jesus (John 14:12)

- I can lay hands on the sick and see them recover (Mark 16:17)

- I can speak in tongues as the Spirit gives me the utterance (Acts 2:4)

- I can cast out evil spirits with authority and power (Mark 16:17)

Appendix F:
Answers to Internalize & Apply Questions

Chapter 1 – How the Father Sees You

1. The Father only sees you as a new creation in Christ, your new man.
2. Because you are co-identified with Christ, your old nature was left in the grave.
3. The Father only deals with your new man because He killed off your old man on the cross and left it in the grace.
4. The Father treats you like He treats Jesus.
5. You are seeking to resurrect your old nature that Jesus killed off at the cross. You are responding from your flesh rather than your born-again spirit.
6. Modifying your behavior seeks to modify your old nature. Instead, the Father gave you a new Christ nature and now reprograms your mind with the mind of Christ to reflect the ways of the new man.
7. True. Your old nature is dead.

Chapter 2 – The Father's Upgrading Process

1. Greater revelation of our identity in Christ, greater revelation of who God is and what He is for us, and an increase in the growth and development of the fruit of the Spirit within us.
2. The Father is spiraling you to higher levels in your identity.
3. God's singular version of you as a righteous son or daughter.
4. Religion, the world system, and our enemy, the devil.

Chapter 3 – Catching Up With Your Spirit

1. Your spiritual mirror is the Word of God, specifically the New Testament, which perfectly reflects who you are in your born-again spirit.
2. Your spirit being was completely transformed when you were born-again, so it is your soul that now needs to be transformed or caught up to your spirit.
3. True. Your soul is not automatically upgraded, it must be activated.

Chapter 4 – Jesus in the Mirror

1. I AM factor: your I AM-ness from God; how the Father made you and sees you.
2. I Am imposter: an inaccurate understanding of who you are as a Christian.
3. Move to I AM factor by reading God's Word to accurately understand who you are in your born-again spirit, and speak it with your mouth.
4. God the Father has the exclusive right to assign a name to me. I should respond by wearing the name that I have been given from my Creator.

Chapter 5 – Perceiving The 'Real' You

1. Spirit, soul, and body
2. No. My flesh (body) or my soul cannot access my human spirit or the spiritual realm.
3. God's Word is the only way to perceive the spirit realm and my human spirit.
4. God's Word perfectly reflects who you are in your born-again spirit.
5. God gave you a new nature (Jesus' nature) in your spirit when you were born again. You are now a new creation.

Chapter 6 – The Activating Valve

1. Your born-again spirit is the 'real' you, the life-giving part of you.
2. God the Father sees your born-again spirit which is as righteous, holy, perfect and complete as Jesus.
3. Renewing your mind and releasing the life of God in your born-again spirit.
4. To agree/cooperate with your born-again spirit to release and experience the life of God; to open the 'valve' to the life of the Spirit.
5. You have the fullness of God in your born-again spirit. As such, God has placed everything you will ever need in your born-again spirit.

Chapter 7 – The Activating Process

1. Activation is the spiritual process of making what is in your born-again spirit become active and operational in your life. It is the process of activating what is in your born-again spirit and planting it into your soul.
2. Hear the word, believe the word, speak the word, and activate (take action on) the word.
3. This means that each word the Lord entrusts to you to carry to completion has an assignment on it. You must live in that word, be fueled by it, steward it, grow it, and believe it. Don't abort it or let the passage of time rob you of God's promise or quench your faith. Don't let that word "fall to the ground."
4. Faith only functions within the heart of a person.
5. A declaration is speaking a truth or a promise of Scripture. A decree, is boldly speaking the purposes of God – something you believe God wants to accomplish that lines up with His will.
6. Your soul — mind, will, and emotions – are in 100% agreement and alignment with what has transpired in your born-again spirit.
7. Words that the Lord quickens and makes alive to you need to intersect with their moment to become completely activated and operational.
8. You activate what God has provided by believing and speaking/declaring the promises of God, which are the 'You saids'.

Chapter 8 – It's a Balancing Act

1. Grace is the unearned, undeserved, and unmerited favor of God toward me, and is 100% what God did for me.
2. When I was born-again, God placed everything I would need in my born-again spirit.
3. False: God's grace is made available to all people whether they receive it or not.
4. Faith is not something that makes God move or do anything.
5. False. Again, faith does not make God do anything.
6. Works, legalism
7. To what God has already provided by grace. It is based on the finished work of Christ on the cross.
8. Activates (appropriates is also acceptable)
9. False. The Christian life is about you responding positively to what He has already done.
10. False. You don't need to plead with God to give you what He has already given through Christ. It's about believing and releasing. You've already got it!

11. Grace and faith must work together to activate what God has already provided.

Chapter 9 – What's True About Your Born-Again Spirit

1. My born-again spirit is the 'real me'.
2. God sees my born-again spirit that is as righteous, holy, perfect, and complete as Jesus. My born-again spirit is as perfect as it will be in eternity.
3. Sin-consciousness: see self as still a sinner at my core. Righteousness consciousness: see self (my identify) as righteous, holy, perfect, and complete as Jesus. Intentionally view myself the way the Father views me.
4. Heart attitude (perspective) of having received the identity of Christ given by our Heavenly Father; to put on and wear the name you have been given; my I AM-ness
5. No, your born-again spirit is not capable of sinning. When you sin, it originates from your flesh (body and soul agreeing), and not from your born-again spirit.

Chapter 10 – The Completeness of Forgiveness

1. No, not an issue between you and God now. God the Father accepted the full payment of His Son on the cross for all your sins – past, present, and future.
2. All my sins – past, present and future – have been forgiven.
3. No. Jesus was offered one time to pay for all my sins – past, present, and the ones I will commit in the future.
4. Heaven. I am righteous and holy in my born-again spirit, and all my sins have been paid for once and for all.

Chapter 11 – The Gift of a Good Conscience

1. Devil, or a defiled conscience
2. Dead works view: that God loves me and accepts me based on my performance – my doing.
   Your conscience is cleansed from "dead works" when you fully accept that Christ's full payment for your sins is what makes you accepted to the Father.
3. Having a sin-consciousness, rather than a righteousness-consciousness.
4. No, my born-again spirit is as holy, clean, pure, and perfect as Jesus. Your spirit is as perfect and complete as it will ever be.

Chapter 12 – An Upgraded View of Repentance

1. It means that you did not practice manifesting the fruit of the Spirit in a situation.
2. You simply confess that you missed the opportunity to be Christ-like, to manifest the fruit of the Spirit.
3. True.

Chapter 13 – Don't Get Hung by Your Tongue

1. Words have creative power, and spoken words create in the natural realm. Everything responds to words that are believed.
2. Words have the effect of a curse when the words are believed or feared.
3. Unforgiveness and hatred will hinder or stop the flow of God's blessings.
4. Biblical meditation means "to mutter" or speak God's Word to yourself. It means to take God's Word and chew on it, to savor it, to ruminate on it, and to speak it.

Chapter 14 – Recircuiting Your Mind

1. The spirit, the conscious mind, and the sub-conscious mind.
2. Agreements or contracts.
3. Agreements cause your sub-conscious mind to rewire the neuropaths in your brain in order to make the new agreement happen.
4. Positive and negative agreements.
5. What lie am I believing about my identity? What's true about my identity?
6. Rejecting and Renouncing the lie followed by Declaring and Announcing what is scripturally true to form a new agreement.

Chapter 15 – "Give Me Back My Stuff"

1. True.
2. No, negativity is a part of your old man, or sin nature.
3. All of your sins and negativity in all its forms – negative thinking, negative behavior, negative emotions, sarcasm, and cynicism.
4. Diagnose the lie, then reject and renounce it, and replace it with the cure – announcing and declaring the truth about your born-again spirit.

5. All negativity is an assault against your identity in Christ. It distracts from your true identity and destiny, distorts how you perceive who you really are in Christ, and challenges the truths God has declared about you.
6. The areas are your *perception* of what's true in your born-again spirit, how you *think* and *feel* about yourself, and how you *talk* about yourself.
7. Attachments come from such sources as the flesh, the world system, and religion.
8. Change the thought to a truth or promise and work on that new thought. Religion tells you to work on the negative thought.
9. True.

Chapter 16 – Let Giants Upgrade You

1. True
2. The three areas are your identity, the fruit of the Spirit being formed in you, and who God is and wants to be for you.
3. That giant is the size I am making you so you are upgraded and elevated for the next season of your life.
4. The WHY question and the WHEN question.
5. The WHAT question followed by the HOW question.
6. God addresses your standing or identity first. Then, you take your upgraded standing into the situation where you think and speak from your new man. You ask the right questions: the WHAT question followed by the HOW question.
7. True.

Chapter 17 – A Soul That Prospers

1. The steps of loosing from your soul, and binding to your soul.
2. True.
3. Negative attachments from wrong agreements.
4. It replaces negative attachments with things that are good and true from scripture about who the Father says you are.
5. True.

Chapter 18 – Shortcuts to an Upgrade

1. It means your circumstances teach you there is a whole new design of you that needs to come out. Your circumstances are accelerating opportunities to grow-up into Christ in all things.
2. Your circumstances are also seated in heaven with you.
3. False. Problems are designed to upgrade you.
4. Possibilities.
5. False. There are only possibilities in heaven.
6. Possibilities.
7. True.

Chapter 19 – An Upgrade of a Different Sort

1. It means Jesus baptizes the believer in the Holy Spirit to receive the Person and power of the Holy Spirit for ministry.
2. The gift of tongues, which is the ability to speak in a heavenly language that you have not learned.
3. The upgrade occurs during the Downloading phase.
4. True.

About the Authors

Dr. Lon Stettler is an ordained minister and educator who is very passionate about discipleship and maturity. He has been very active in the discipleship ministry for over four decades. Lon has written, preached, and taught discipleship courses for more than thirty years. He holds a Doctor of Philosophy degree from Miami University in educational leadership and served as a school district administrator for 26 years.

Laurie is a mother of four children and retired high school teacher who assists with disciplining women. She and Lon have seven wonderful grandchildren.

Lon and Laurie currently live near Charleston, South Carolina. Contact: lon.stettler@gmail.com

CPSIA information can be obtained
at www.ICGtesting.com
Printed in the USA
BVHW021501280323
661291BV00006B/202